Starting Skills in English

Listening and Speaking
Part A

Teacher's Book

Terry Phillips

Published by
Garnet Publishing Ltd.
8 Southern Court
South Street
Reading RG1 4QS, UK

Copyright © 2005 Garnet Publishing Ltd.

The right of Terry Phillips to be identified as the author of this work has been asserted by him in accordance with the Copyright, Designs and Patents Act 1988.

All rights reserved.
No part of this publication may be reproduced, stored in a retrieval system, or transmitted in any form or by any means, electronic, mechanical, photocopying, recording or otherwise, without the prior permission of the Publisher. Any person who does any unauthorized act in relation to this publication may be liable to criminal prosecution and civil claims for damages.

This edition first published 2005

ISBN 1 85964 804 5

British Library Cataloguing-in-Publication Data
A catalogue record for this book is available from the British Library.

Production
Project managers: Richard Peacock, Francesca Pinagli
Editorial team: Rod Webb, Lucy Thompson
Art director: David Rose
Typesetting: Samantha Barden
Illustration: Doug Nash, Karen Rose
  Beehive Illustration: (Colin Brown /
  Janos Jantner / Martin Sanders /
  Laszlo Veres)
Photography: Banana Stock, Corbis, Digital Vision,
  Flat Earth, Image Source,
  Ingram Publishing, Photodisc, Stockbyte

Garnet Publishing wishes to thank the following for their assistance in the piloting of this project:
David Anderson, Kaye Anderson, Alec Benson, Terry Boucher, William Davis, Jeanette Drissi, Patrick Flavin, Bruce Gunn, Marion King, Leslie Kirkham, Nicholas Lake, Mairead Lyons-Hackett, Peter Newbery, Barbara Mary Rowell, Roland Steinwand, Evan Sullivan, Yusuf Suluh, Kevin Watson, Debra Wedl, John Wells and teachers and administrators from the Higher Colleges of Technology in the UAE.

Special thanks go to Nicola Marsden and Hinemoa Xhori.

Every effort has been made to trace the copyright holders and we apologize in advance for any unintentional omissions. We will be happy to insert the appropriate acknowledgements in any subsequent editions.

Audio production: Chris Dalby, YellowPark

Printed and bound
in Lebanon by International Press

Contents

Book Map	4
Introduction	6
Starter	12
Theme 1: *Work and Business*	38
Theme 2: *Science and Nature*	50
Theme 3: *The Physical World*	66
Theme 4: *Culture and Civilization*	78
Theme 5: *They Made Our World*	92
Theme 6: *Art and Literature*	108
Theme 7: *Sports and Leisure*	124
Theme 8: *Nutrition and Health*	138
Word Lists	
Thematic	152
Alphabetical	154

Starting Skills in English
Listening and Speaking
Part A

Book Map

Listening (Lessons 1 and 3)	Speaking (Lessons 2 and 4)
Starter	
• target words in isolation • target words in context • predicting next word • hearing /e/, /ɪ/ and /aɪ/ • instructions for classwork • recognising target questions	• target words in isolation • target words in context • asking target questions • saying /e/, /ɪ/ and /aɪ/ • introducing self (1): age, name, nationality, hometown

Listening (Lessons 1 and 2)	Speaking (Lessons 3 and 4)
Theme 1 – Work and Business	
• target words in isolation • target words in context • hearing /ɑː/ and /eɪ/ • identifying key factual information	• target words in isolation • target words in context • saying /ɑː/ and /eɪ/ • asking target questions • introducing self (2): job, date of birth
Theme 2 – Science and Nature	
• target words in isolation • target words in context • hearing /iː/ • understanding descriptions (1)	• target words in isolation • target words in context • saying *can* and *can't* • asking about abilities • asking target questions • describing objects
Theme 3 – The Physical World	
• target words in isolation • target words in context • hearing /aʊ/ • understanding descriptions (2)	• target words in isolation • target words in context • saying /aʊ/ • asking target questions • describing places

Listening (Lessons 1 and 2)	Speaking (Lessons 3 and 4)
Theme 4 – Culture and Civilization	
• target words in isolation • target words in context • hearing /æ/	• target words in isolation • target words in context • asking about new words • the letter *a* • stress within words
Theme 5 – They Made Our World	
• target words in isolation • target words in context • predicting information • hearing /əʊ/	• target words in isolation • target words in context • defining things • saying /əʊ/ and /aʊ/
Theme 6 – Art and Literature	
• target words in isolation • target words in context • preparing to listen: the introduction • guessing information • hearing /ə/ at the end of words	• target words in isolation • target words in context • saying /ə/ at the end of words • talking about the past
Theme 7 – Sports and Leisure	
• target words in isolation • target words in context • predicting the next word or phrase • hearing /ɒ/ and /ɔː/	• target words in isolation • target words in context • talking about figures: bar charts • saying /ɒ/ and /ɔː/
Theme 8 – Nutrition and Health	
• target words in isolation • target words in context • listening for examples • hearing /uː/ and /ʊ/	• target words in isolation • target words in context • doing research: preparing to ask questions • saying /uː/ and /ʊ/

INTRODUCTION

Why is *Starting Skills in English* different?

Starting Skills in English is designed exclusively for teenage and young adult false beginners. Many courses claim to be suitable for this target group, but do not consider the real profile of their target students.

- False beginners are *not* true beginners. They are people with a great deal of passive knowledge, especially of vocabulary, in whom later learning has driven out earlier basic points. *Starting Skills in English* systematises this previous learning so it can become genuinely useful.
- False beginners are *not* effective language learners who have simply forgotten previous learning. Therefore, they will not benefit, in the main, from a revision course with a very fast syllabus progression. They need a course which lock-steps them through each point, to ensure that they understand it before moving on.
- *Starting Skills in English* takes students step by step through the basic points they should have learnt before and demonstrates the communicative value of lexical, grammatical, orthographic and phonological points.
- False beginners, in many cases, are *not* read-write learners. They have struggled with the text-heavy materials in many school course books. They may be visual learners, who need colour and pictures, or aural learners, who need sounds and repetition. They may even be kinaesthetic learners who need to touch things and move them around to make sense of them. *Starting Skills in English* recognises different learning styles and gives students different ways of learning the same information.
- False beginners, in many cases, are *not* inductive learners. They have struggled to learn with the methodology of example to rule. They need to be given the opportunity to learn deductively as well, from rule – or perhaps we should say, pattern – to example. *Starting Skills in English* often gives students two routes – an inductive and a deductive way – with the use of overt *Skills Check* boxes for the deductive learner and activities for the inductive learner.
- False beginners, in the main, have no desire to go 'right back to the beginning'. They may have low motivation to study English anyway, given their history of failure, but they will certainly not be motivated by things that even they find too easy or, at least, too familiar. *Starting Skills in English* aims to teach old points in a new way.
- As mentioned before, false beginners have, to some extent, failed previous learning. They have sat in classes for, perhaps, nine years, but they are still not able to pass a formal test of English at more than beginner level. This means they need to be convinced that they can succeed this time. *Starting Skills in English* aims to give success right from the start, with materials which are interesting and challenging for students but within their grasp.
- False beginners in a class are *not* an homogenous group. For any given item of beginner- / elementary-level vocabulary or grammar, there will be someone in the group who knows the item and many others who do not. But the 'knower' will change from item to item. *Starting Skills in English* acknowledges previous successful learning and, at the same time, enables the teacher to see which students are struggling on a particular point so he / she can direct those students to the additional remedial work provided.
- False beginners can do very little with the language, even in areas where they have some knowledge. In other words, they have some competence but few or no specific performance skills in listening, speaking, reading or writing which they will need for further study in English. *Starting Skills in English* introduces students to key points in the four skills.

What is the structure of *Starting Skills in English*?

Starting Skills in English is divided into two parts, A and B. Students can enter the course at A or B level. Each part provides at least 150 hours' tuition. The whole course, therefore, provides at least 300 hours' tuition.

There are three books in each part.
1 *Listening and Speaking*
2 *Reading and Writing*
3 *Vocabulary and Grammar*

The third book is linked to exercises on the dedicated *Starting Skills in English* website.

It is assumed that most users of the course will teach the books in this order, although it is not essential. The majority of the material in the third book, *Vocabulary and Grammar*, could be set as self-study.

Each of the three books contains ten themes, based on the *Encyclopaedia Britannica* organisation of human knowledge. This means that students learn useful, transferable content as well as useful transferable vocabulary and skills as they work through the course. *Starting Skills in English* does not assume that graduates from the course are going to become world travellers, using English as a lingua franca. Instead, it assumes they are going on to further study in English. Therefore, the themes covered build knowledge and skills which will assist in further English-medium study.

The ten themes are:
1 Education
2 Daily Life
3 Work and Business
4 Science and Nature
5 The Physical World
6 Culture and Civilization
7 Technology and Inventions
8 Art and Literature
9 Sports and Leisure
10 Nutrition and Health

Note that in Part A, the first two themes are combined into a Starter section. This section provides revision of very low-level items which all students should know well.

Work within each theme is, therefore, constrained by a lexical set. This means that students gain in confidence in using a limited set of lexical items as they work through the theme, rather than constantly having to cope with new words which happen to appear in presentation texts.

Starting Skills in English recognises that there is more to knowing a word than knowing its base meaning, and so by the end of each theme, students should be confident in using words in written or spoken form and proficient at recognising the word in both forms. They will often also know some common collocations of words in a theme and important grammatical points about words, such as plural formation.

What is the approach of *Starting Skills in English*?

Starting Skills in English adopts a recurrent structure within each theme. This is broadly a Test–Teach–Test approach, which appears to be the best to accommodate all the needs of false beginners as previously detailed. In other words, students are first tested, informally, on the English they know in a particular area. There is then a range of teaching activities to ensure full competence in that area, then a final test, again informal, of the same points. It is worth pointing out that students may not notice the informal testing, since it is not flagged as a test except in Grammar. This is not a problem, since the main aim is to show teachers what students know / do not know, although it can also be motivating for students to realise that they need to learn particular items from a lexical set or a particular skill or grammar point.

The main part of the course is organised into themes. The same theme is used across the three books in Part A. Within each theme, there are four lessons.

Listening and Speaking and Reading and Writing

In each theme, **Lesson 1** is a test or deep-end strategy lesson on the receptive skills, listening or reading, in a particular theme area. Hopefully, students will get most items right in this lesson, thus confirming their false beginner (rather than true beginner) status. If they do, they will end with a page full of motivating ticks. However, teachers are encouraged to make a note of students who get specific items wrong and to try to ensure that, by the end of Lesson 2, they are getting those items right.

Lesson 2 highlights and does remedial work on the receptive skill points in Lesson 1. In this lesson there is also some productive work, in speaking or writing, of words and sentences that have been highlighted to date.

Lesson 3 is a test or deep-end strategy lesson on the related productive skill, speaking or writing, in a particular theme area. The purpose is the same as Lesson 1 – to motivate students and highlight points for remedial work. Once again, teachers are encouraged to make a note of students who get specific items wrong and try to ensure by the end of Lesson 4 they are getting that item right.

Lesson 4 highlights and does remedial work on the speaking or writing points in Lesson 3.

Note that this pattern becomes clearer as the course proceeds. Lessons 1 and 2 of the Starter section of Part A, for example, do not exhibit all these features.

Vocabulary and Grammar

As with the other two books, **Lesson 1** is a test or deep-end strategy lesson on vocabulary in a particular theme area. Teachers are encouraged to make a note of students who get specific items wrong and follow one or more of these courses of action:

a work with them individually during the lesson
b work with small groups of students having the same problem during the lesson
c refer students to remedial vocabulary work on the website.

Whatever action is taken, the students should be retested afterwards to demonstrate that they have made progress.

In Lesson 1 in Part A, there is one or more exercise in each theme on numbers, in addition to thematically-linked work. *Starting Skills in English* believes that proficiency with using numbers in speech and in writing is central to English-medium study and therefore devotes a considerable amount of time to this point, dealing with it systematically.

Lesson 2 covers more ground using a test / deep-end strategy. In many cases there is a lexical grammar issue to be dealt with, such as singular and plural. In this lesson, Skills Checks highlight points for specific learning.

In Lesson 2 in Part A, there is one or more exercise on the correct form of letters in English, and later on, alphabetical order, for students from an exotic language.

Lesson 3 is a test or deep-end strategy lesson on grammar in a particular area. The purpose is the same as Lesson 1. Teachers are encouraged to note students who get specific items wrong. On this occasion, however, the remedial work is directly provided in Lesson 4. Students should therefore be tested again after they have completed this lesson to see if they have improved on weak items.

Lesson 4 highlights and does remedial work on the grammar points in Lesson 3. If students are still struggling with these grammar points after the lesson, they should be referred to the website / CD for further remedial work.

Key activities

Vocabulary learning in general

Starting Skills in English believes that the key to good language learning is the acquisition of a broad, useful, transferable vocabulary. As mentioned before, vocabulary learning is not just about meaning. It is also about form in speech and writing and about collocation and usage.

Starting Skills in English looks at a lexical set in each theme in each of the four skills in turn. Firstly, students are taught to hear the set of words, in isolation and in context. They are then given the opportunity to produce the same set of words in speech, in isolation and context. Then the same set of words is flashed at them, to improve the ability to recognise the word in written form at high speed. The words are then included in a variety of texts for recognition in context. Finally, students are given the opportunity to prove their ability to produce the same set of words in writing, with the correct spelling and usage.

Listening

Listen and point

This may look like a primary-level activity, but it is the best way to prove ability to relate objects and action verbs to the sound of the words, in isolation and the stream of speech, without having to engage in any other linguistic activity, e.g., speaking or writing. It greatly aids the aural learner and, because there is a physical element, may assist the kinaesthetic learner.

Listen and do

This TPR (Total Physical Response) activity may also look like a primary-level activity, but it is the best way to prove ability to relate spoken language to its communicative purpose without a linguistic output. It greatly aids the kinaesthetic learner.

Listen and tick the next word

A key listening skill is the ability to predict the next word. It is part of the hypothesis checking of active listening. We can only cope with the speed of incoming data in the stream of speech if we have to some extent predicted the content.

Listen and draw

This is another way of checking understanding without a linguistic output.

Skills Checks – hearing specific phonemes

How can a student recognise a word in the stream of speech if he / she cannot recognise the phonemes it contains? *Starting Skills in English* presents discrete phonemes then phonemes in contrast, and checks the students' ability to hear, then discriminate.

Skills Checks – listening skills

Students are taught to listen for important words – a key skill.

Speaking

Look and name

This is the converse of *Listen and point*. At this point, the teacher can focus on ensuring that students can correctly name depicted items and make a reasonable approximation of the pronunciation.

Listen and look

Although this may appear to be a listening activity, it is actually an essential precursor to speaking. Students are usually given the opportunity to hear a conversation before reading it. This greatly helps aural learners, and ensures for all learners that there is an aural trace of sounds in their brain, which they can recover to help with their own pronunciation.

Work in pairs – information gap

Activities often involve an information gap – one student has information and the other has to close the gap.

Work in pairs – role play

Students are given the opportunity to practise transactional conversations which they have previously heard. This assists aural learners.

Work in pairs – talk about yourself

Students are given the opportunity to talk about themselves, using the patterns they have practised in a preceding role play.

Talk about yourself

This is often a development from *Work in pairs – talk about yourself*. Students are taught to take the individual sentences from the pairwork and turn them into a connected text for an oral presentation.

Ask and answer

This activity often contains dessicated sentences, i.e., sentences which only retain the function words. This kind of exercise probably mimics the production of sentences in the human brain. It is likely that we retrieve the content words first, then the function words which carry them in a given sentence.

Rebus conversations

A rebus is a picture which prompts a word or a sentence. It is a child's puzzle, but it is used in *Starting Skills in English* because it mimics real-world language production. We store meanings above linguistic level, then translate them into words. Thus, a picture of a map of England plus a question mark can prompt the question *Are you from England?*

This probably assists all learners, but especially visual learners.

Skills Checks – saying specific phonemes
Starting Skills in English presents discrete phonemes for accurate production then phonemes in contrast, and checks the students' ability to say and / or discriminate. These Skills Checks often point out common sound-sight relationships, e.g., *ow* may be /aʊ/ or /ə/.

Reading
The texts
The majority of texts in *Starting Skills in English* are simulated authentic – in other words, they are pieces of written English that a student might actually encounter in their daily life or might have to read for their studies. The principal activities based on those texts are real-world – in other words, things that a person might really have to do while reading or after reading such a text. In addition, there are often analytical tasks which help students to recognise key points about the form or organisation of information in the text which will help them to read similar texts in the future.

Look and read
The teacher flashes words from the lexical set for students to recognise in written form. Response is in speech and one could argue that this is wrong as it requires a linguistic response. However, by this point, students have had the opportunity to produce the target words in speech on many occasions, so spoken response should, on the one hand, not be a challenge, and on the other, should provide a good revision of oral production.

Skills Checks – reading skills
Students are taken step by step through key reading skills, including basic points related to the decoding of written text.

Find and circle / underline / box
Students are required to annotate written text to show they can correctly identify key features of punctuation and recognise key parts of speech – noun, verb and adjective. This understanding of parts of speech is fundamental to being able to guess the meaning of a new word in context. If you do not know what part of speech it is, it will be very hard to guess the meaning.

Right or wrong?
Reading is made communicative from the very beginning. Students are asked to look at visual prompts and recognise whether sentences correctly describe what they see.

Writing
The tasks
The majority of writing tasks involve the production of real-world texts – in other words, pieces of connected prose that students might have to do as part of their English studies at a later date, rather than simply sentence-level manipulation of grammatical points.

Crosswords
These are an excellent way of checking a student's ability to name real items or recognise what is missing from a sentence, and produce the word with correct spelling. They are particularly useful for learners with a high tolerance of ambiguity.

Tick the correct sentences
Writing is made communicative from the very beginning. Students are asked to look at visual prompts and choose the correct sentence to describe what they see.

Read and complete
This usually involves the identification of the missing vowel, because in English consonants are largely phonemic (sound = sight) whereas vowels are not. If students write the correct vowels in a word, the chances are the word will be correctly spelt.

Number the boxes in order
English is a syntagmatic language – in other words, meaning is largely carried by the order of words rather

than by paradigms which indicate case or gender. Therefore, students need constant practice in putting words in an acceptable 'English' order. In *Starting Skills in English*, most sentences are based on the S V (C) (O) (A) pattern.

Skills Checks – spelling
These checks teach common patterns of sound-sight.

Skills Checks – writing skills
This is sometimes the converse of the Reading Skills Checks. For instance, students are asked to identify the capitalised words in Reading, then to add the capitals in the related Writing section. At other times, the Writing Skills Checks cover points which are not important to the reader but vital to the writer. In particular, many of these checks cover points of grammaticised lexis such as the use of determiners with different kinds of nouns.

Vocabulary
General
It is assumed that students come to the lessons in a particular theme having studied the lexical set in speech and writing in the other two books. Therefore, there is a combination of listening (to the teacher), speaking, reading and writing in these lessons.

Number work
As mentioned before, there are many exercises, in Part A particularly, on numbers. By the end of this course, students should be fully proficient with the complexities of this important, and often under-practised, issue.

Alphabet work
Students who come from a language with a different alphabet often struggle for years to recognise key features of English orthography and to reproduce them in their own writing. These exercises take such students step by step through these vital features. In later themes in Part A, alphabetical order is explained and practised.

Wordsearch
This is an excellent way to check a student's ability to pick out word shapes. It is well-known now that good readers recognise words from their complete pattern rather than by decoding individual letters and then assembling them.

Collocation
A key point about words – 'we know them by the company they keep'. (Fries)

Synonymy, Antonym, Hyponymy, Hypernymy / Superordination
These are key points about semantic relationships between words, vital for lexical cohesion work later in their learning. For example, students must recognise that a *car* is a *vehicle*, otherwise they may not understand that the writer is referring to the same item even though she / he uses the two different words.

Grammar
Tests
These are diagnostic tests. Each item relates to one of the sentence or phrase patterns points in Lesson 4. Students and teacher alike can see points of difficulty at a glance.

Parallel production
Many themes contain this kind of task, where students are asked to use a model text to create a text of a similar nature about a different subject, or where information is transferred from, e.g., table to text, and back again.

Sentence / phrase patterns
English is an S V (O) (A) language. Students need to gain a firm grasp of this concept and to understand what can fit into each of the categories. The sentence / phrase patterns in this section build into an invaluable compendium of this basic structure, which should ensure that students are confident to build from this to compound and complex sentences in later courses.

Colour coding is used in these sentence patterns. This greatly assists all students to match function and form in the pattern but is, of course, of especial value to the visual learner.

STARTER STRUCTURE

The book begins with a *Starter* section. This section covers very familiar vocabulary from the areas of education and daily life. Make it clear to students that this is revision. There are four lessons in this section, each occupying a double-page spread of the course book. However, with a strong class you could go even faster. You might even decide to omit this section completely, just checking the vocabulary in a quick oral activity.

Lesson 1 (page 6) is a test or deep-end strategy lesson on listening in a particular theme area (Education). Hopefully, students will get most items right, proving their false-beginner status. If they do, they will end with a page full of motivating ticks. However, make a note of students who get specific items wrong and try to ensure they are getting that item right by the end of Lesson 1.

Lesson 1 (page 7) highlights and does remedial work on the listening points on page 6. There is also some speaking in this lesson of words and sentences that have been highlighted to date.

Lesson 2 (page 8) is a test or deep-end-strategy lesson on speaking in a particular theme area (Daily Life). The purpose is the same as Lesson 1. Make a note of students who get specific items wrong and try to ensure they are getting those items right by the end of Lesson 2.

Lesson 2 (page 9) highlights and does remedial work on the speaking points on page 8.

STARTER Education Daily Life

General note

By the end of the Starter section, students should be able to hear and identify, in isolation and in context, the following words linked with education and daily life. They should also be able to say the words with reasonable pronunciation and use them in very simple imperative sentences (*Open your book.*), S V (*be*) C sentences (*I am Spanish. / I'm from Beijing.*) and S V O sentences (*Lesson 4 is at 1.*).

Education

answer (*n* and *v*)	listen	student
ask	question (*n*)	test (*n*)
begin	read	write
end (*v*)	right	wrong

Daily Life

afternoon	hour	now
date	last	time
day	month	today
evening	morning	week
first	night	year

In addition, students should be able to hear and say the months of the year, the days of the week and numbers from *1* to *20*. False-beginner students should be reasonably confident with these items, although they may still have problems with pronunciation and spelling; in addition, they may not understand how certain numbers, especially ordinals, are constructed and abbreviated.

Lesson 1: Listening

Introduction

Introduce yourself and say hello to the students. Use the target questions from later in Starter, i.e.,

Hello. How are you?
What's your name?
Are you English?
Do we need this?
We've got ...
Are you a student?
Where are you from? (eliciting nationality or hometown)

Move on to another student if some are unable or unwilling to answer. Hopefully, you will be able to elicit correct answers from a number of students, which will serve as exemplars to the weaker students.

Exercise A

Begin with student books closed. Hold up a book and say *book*. Do not ask students to repeat, but do not stop them if they wish to. Point to a desk and say *desk*. Say *book* again, and indicate that you want students to point to their books. Repeat the procedure with *desk*. When you think students understand the activity, say all the other words in Exercise A, or play the tape. Watch the students and try to identify any student who is not correctly associating with the spoken word and the object.

This is the list of target words.
  book
  desk
  chair
  door
  classroom
  teacher
  student
  pen
  pencil
  board

Tapescript

Presenter:	Starter
	Lesson 1
	A Listen and point.
Voice:	book
	desk
	chair
	door
	classroom
	teacher
	student
	pen
	pencil
	board

You can go through this activity as many times as you wish, speeding up and saying the words in a different order. After you have said the words in isolation a few times, start to say the words in context as follows. Exaggerate the target content words slightly.

> *Open your book.*
> *Which is your desk?*
> *Can you give me a chair?*
> *There's someone at the door.*
> *Is this your classroom?*
> *What's the name of your teacher?*
> *Are you a student?*
> *Could you lend me a pen?*
> *I've only got a pencil.*
> *OK. Can you look at the board?*

Methodology notes

1. With large classes, put the students into pairs or small groups to check that they are pointing at the correct word each time. Remember. This is a self-check, largely for students to prove that they can identify the words in isolation and context, so do not worry if you cannot tell from your position.
2. Remember! Lesson 1 of this theme focuses mainly on listening, so do not spend a lot of time on speaking. We know that listening helps speaking. It is less certain that speaking helps listening, so save the speaking practice for Lesson 2.
3. Some of your students will be kinaesthetic learners. Encourage students to get up and go and touch things if they wish (while you are saying the words in isolation), rather than pointing at them.
4. Hearing words in isolation is much easier than hearing them in context. However, it is not a very valuable real-world skill. Whenever you have checked that students can hear a word in isolation, put it into a context. This encourages students to develop the vital listening skill of picking key words out from the stream of speech.

Language and culture note

Pointing with the index finger is rude in many cultures, including in English-speaking countries. Avoid any student reticence to point by using an open-handed gesture rather than an index finger.

Exercise B

Make it clear that you are moving on to another activity. Get the attention of all the students. Say the first instruction from the list below. Do the first one for the students as an example. Wait until a student does it. Repeat until all the students have opened their books. Continue with the next two or three instructions. Say each one once and wait, then repeat until everybody is doing it. When students understand the activity, go through all the instructions or play the tape, then go through them again at random, getting faster.

This is the complete list of instructions.

> *Open your book.*
> *Look at page 10.*
> *Read the first sentence.*
> *Close your book.*
> *Look at the board.*
> *Open your notebook.*
> *Write your name.*
> *Write your phone number.*
> *Stand up.*
> *Sit down.*

Tapescript

Presenter: B Listen and do.
Voice: Open your book.
Look at page 10.
Read the first sentence.
Close your book.
Look at the board.
Open your notebook.
Write your name.
Write your phone number.
Stand up.
Sit down.

Methodology notes

1. Keep control of the cassette / CD so that you can give plenty of time for students to do the required actions.
2. This activity is a form of Total Physical Response (TPR). TPR is valuable because:
   - in a listening lesson, it does not require another linguistic skill in the response as, e.g., *listen and repeat* or *listen and answer* does.
   - it helps kinaesthetic learners to remember words and phrases.
   - it clearly indicates to the teacher who understands and who does not.
3. Some students – and teachers – might be embarrassed at first by this type of activity. Try to overcome their (your) resistance, as it is another invaluable learning tool.

Exercise C

Once again, make it clear that you have moved on to another activity. Ask the first question in the list below. Wait for an answer from someone. Confirm or wait for a correct answer. Continue with the next question. When students understand the activity, go through all the questions or play the tape, then go through them again at random, getting faster. Do not pick on individual students, but note any who are struggling.

This is the complete list of questions.
What's your name?
Are you English?
Are you at school?
Are you a student?
What class are you in?
Is your teacher American?
What's the name of your book?

Tapescript

Presenter: C Listen and answer.
Voice: What's your name?
Are you English?
Are you at school?
Are you a student?
What class are you in?
Is your teacher American?
What's the name of your book?

Methodology note

Even in real life we would not necessarily expect a full answer. In a listening lesson, it is sufficient that a student has understood the questions. Do not worry about the form of the answer or the pronunciation. You can focus on that in Lesson 2.

Exercise D

Say *Open your book. Look at page 6. Look at A. Listen and point.* Repeat the activity, walking around the class and checking individual students. Tick the words they get right. Try to ensure that you catch people doing things right!

> **Methodology note**
>
> If students are struggling with numbers *1–10*, they are covered in the *Vocabulary and Grammar* book.

Closure

Give one of the instructions to a good student, e.g., *Close your book*. When he / she does it correctly, say *OK, you can go. Goodbye*. Indicate that the student can leave the room. Continue with at least 10 or 12 students at random – the point, of course, is that they have to get the action right to be allowed to leave the class!

Lesson 1: Listening

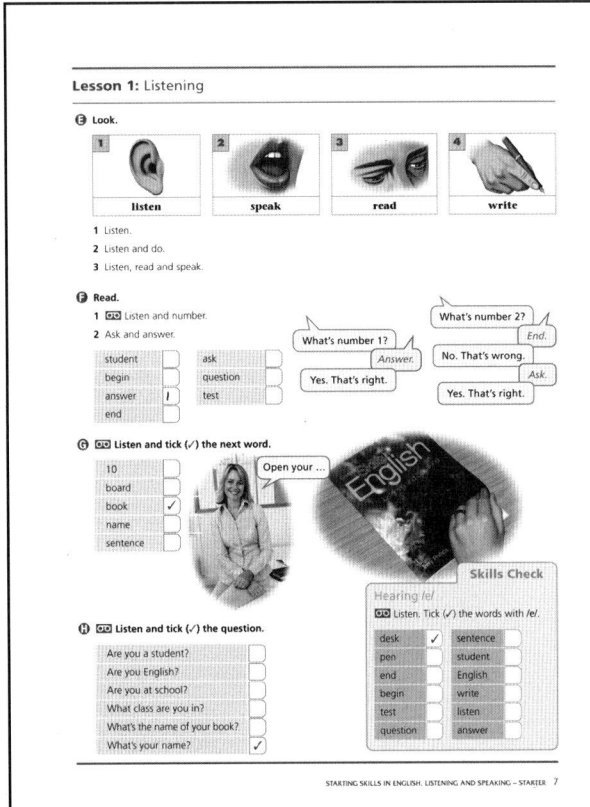

Introduction

Go through some of the words in isolation and context, and some of the TPR instructions from the previous lesson.

Exercise E

1. Point to your ear and say *Listen*. Point to your mouth and, after a pause to see if anyone is going to say anything, say *Speak*. Point to your eyes and mime reading something and, after a pause, say *Read*. Mime writing and, after a pause, say *Write*. Go through the activity once more.
2. Reverse the activity, i.e., you say one of the words and the students have to mime it. Repeat a few times, saying the words in isolation at random, then in context, e.g.,
   Write your name.
   Read the sentence.
   Listen to the CD.
   Could you speak more slowly?
   Make sure students realise they only have to mime the action, not do it.
3. Say *Open your book* and indicate that students really have to do this. Refer them to the four pictures. Say *Listen,* then say *Read number 1.* When a student has correctly responded, repeat the command several times and elicit the word *Listen* from several other students. Continue with the other numbers in order, then again at random.

Methodology note

The last part of this activity looks like, and is, a reading activity. However, this is a listening lesson! The apparent anomaly is because an important sub-skill of listening is relating the sound and the sight of a word. This is especially problematic in English, which is not a phonemic language, i.e., you cannot always work out the sound of a word from the way that it is spelt. Students sometimes fail to identify in speech a word which they can read, so this type of activity ensures that the brain makes the correct sound-sight relationship and enables speedy identification of the word.

Exercise F

1. Refer students to the list of words. Give them a few moments to look at the words. Do not let students speak. Say the first word, or play the tape of the first word. Show that students must write the number after the word. Continue with the second word. Set for individual work and pairwork checking. Say or play the rest of the words. Do not feedback at this point.
2. This activity ensures that students understand and can use the words *right* and *wrong*. Refer students to the speech bubbles. Work through the mini-conversations, Teacher-Students, then half the

class, then open pairs. Set for pairwork. Monitor and assist.

Feed back, saying the words in order, and eliciting the numbers.

Answers

student	6
begin	3
answer	1
end	4
ask	2
question	5
test	7

Tapescript

Presenter: F 1 Listen and number.
Voice: 1 answer
2 ask
3 begin
4 end
5 question
6 student
7 test

Methodology notes

1 Demonstratives are revised later in the course, but it is perfectly acceptable to teach their use (as in *That's right.*) in a fixed phrase. Native speakers are not really using the word *that* with deictic reference any more. They are just producing a learnt phrase, and you can teach your students to do the same.

2 If you are working in a situation where students might actually need to use English immediately outside the classroom, end this activity by pointing out that *That's wrong* is not polite. You can demonstrate this by saying it loudly and 'rudely'. Teach them the alternative (as a fixed phrase) *I don't think that's right.*

Exercise G

Refer students to the picture. Say the words in the speech bubble. Ask students to guess the next word. The tick in the list of words is a helpful clue! Say or play the next sentence and elicit the correct next word. Continue to confirm. Say or play the rest of the sentences. Do not let students speak, only tick. Play the whole activity again for students to compare answers.

Answers

1 Open your *book*.
2 Look at page *10*.
3 Read the first *sentence*.
4 Look at the *board*.
5 Write your *name*.

Tapescript

Presenter: G Listen and tick the next word.
Female tutor: Open your [PAUSE] book.
Look at page [PAUSE] 10.
Read the first [PAUSE] sentence.
Look at the [PAUSE] board.
Write your [PAUSE] name.

Methodology note

When we listen, we make hypotheses all the time about what the person is going to say next. This even extends to the next word or phrase. Without these hypotheses, we probably could not listen efficiently because we would have to wait for each incoming word or phrase before we tried to understand – and then we would miss the next bit of incoming data. We must teach students this vital sub-skill in L2, or they will never be efficient listeners.

Exercise H

Set for individual work and pairwork checking. Say or play the example. Continue with the rest of the questions. Do not ask students to listen and repeat the questions at this stage. The focus is still on listening and understanding, not on listening so that you can say the words.

Tapescript

Presenter:	H Listen and tick the question.
Female tutor:	What's your name?
	Are you English?
	Are you at school?
	Are you a student?
	What class are you in?
	What's the name of your book?

> **Methodology note**
>
> This is another version of Exercise G. We must identify a question very quickly in interactive listening so that we can answer appropriately.

Skills Check

A number of words in this theme have the /e/ sound rendered by the letter *e*. This is, of course, not the only way to render /e/, viz., *said, many*, but it is the most common.

Do not ask the students to listen and repeat – just say the sound in isolation and then in *desk* and *pen*, so that students begin to train their ear to hear it. Write the symbol /e/ on the board and demonstrate that you can find this kind of symbol in a dictionary.

Set for individual work and pairwork checking. Say or play the words. Feed back by building up the table on the board. Do not worry about the sounds in the other words except as indicated in the Answers below; it is sufficient that students can hear that they are not /e/.

Tapescript

Presenter:	Skills Check
	Listen. Tick the words with /e/.
Voice:	desk
	pen
	end
	begin
	test
	question
	sentence
	student
	English
	write
	listen
	answer

Answers

See the table on page 11.

Closure

Say goodbye to the students, pausing before predictable words to see if anyone can guess what you are going to say next, e.g.,

OK. That's the end of the [PAUSE] *lesson.*
I will see you [PAUSE] (whenever is correct) *at* (whenever is correct).
Your next lesson is [PAUSE] (whatever is correct).

word	/e/	notes
desk	✓	
pen	✓	
end	✓	
begin		
test	✓	
question	✓	
sentence	✓	the first *e*
student		
English		
write		Point out that the *e* has no sound in this position. Elicit other words from this lesson with *e* in this position, e.g., *name, where, are.*
listen		Point out that *t* has no sound in this word.
answer		Point out that *er* makes the schwa sound /ə/, but do not use the word. Elicit other words from this lesson with *er* in this position, e.g., *teacher, number.*

Lesson 2: Speaking

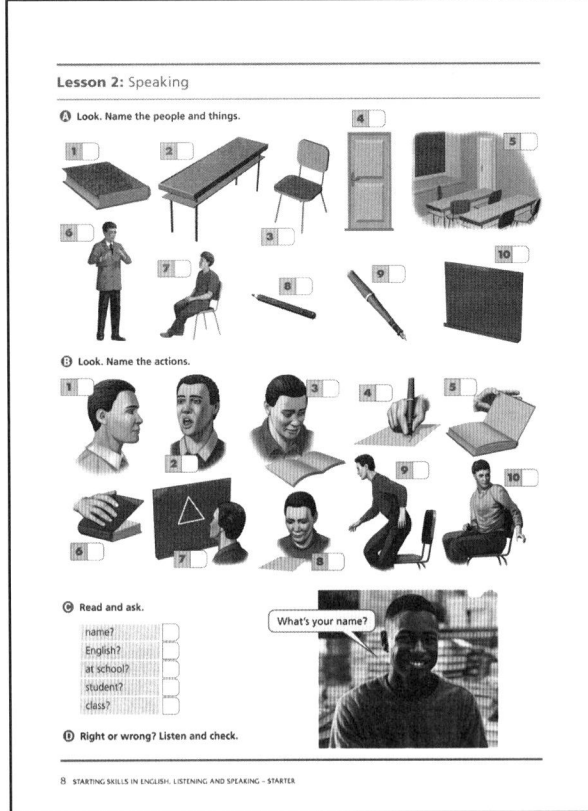

Methodology note

The course focuses on general problems of phoneme production. If you are aware of problems with specific phonemes from your students or a particular speech group among your students, take any opportunity to do some extra work on one or more of those points. Here, for example, you can contrast:
/p/ and /b/
/l/ and /r/ in *classroom*
the clusters *cl* and *st*, getting, e.g., Spanish speakers not to put a preceding vowel.

Exercise B

Repeat the same procedure as Exercise A. Target student output is the imperative, i.e., *Listen*. Monitor and assist. As before, make a note of anyone struggling and give extra help.

Introduction

Point to things in the classroom and get students to name them. Point to yourself and then to one student at the end.

Exercise A

Refer students to the illustrations. Put them in pairs to identify and say the items. Monitor and make a note of any students who are struggling. Give extra help now or later. Feed back, getting students to give themselves ticks if they can identify the words and say them reasonably correctly. On this occasion, focus on the /e/ sound and on words with the letter *e* which do not have the /e/ sound.

Exercise C

Write the question *What's your name?* on the board. Underline the word *name* to show that this is the key word. Elicit the other questions from the key words in the list. Drill the questions, i.e.,

    You say: *name?*
      Ss say: *What's your name?*
    You say: *English?*
      etc.

Remember to give the key word the correct intonation pattern, i.e., fall or fall-rise. Back-chain, if necessary. Set for pairwork. Monitor and assist, noting problems.

> **Methodology note**
>
> It is likely that we begin the process of creating a question with a key word, e.g., we want to ask for someone's name and we get the word *name* first, then remember how to form the question. This exercise therefore mimics a real-life speaking skill.

Exercise D

Go through the whole page once more, encouraging students to give themselves a tick for each one they can do successfully. Tell students to work on the ones they got wrong in their own time.

Closure

Put students into pairs to give each other instructions as in Exercise B.

Lesson 2: Speaking

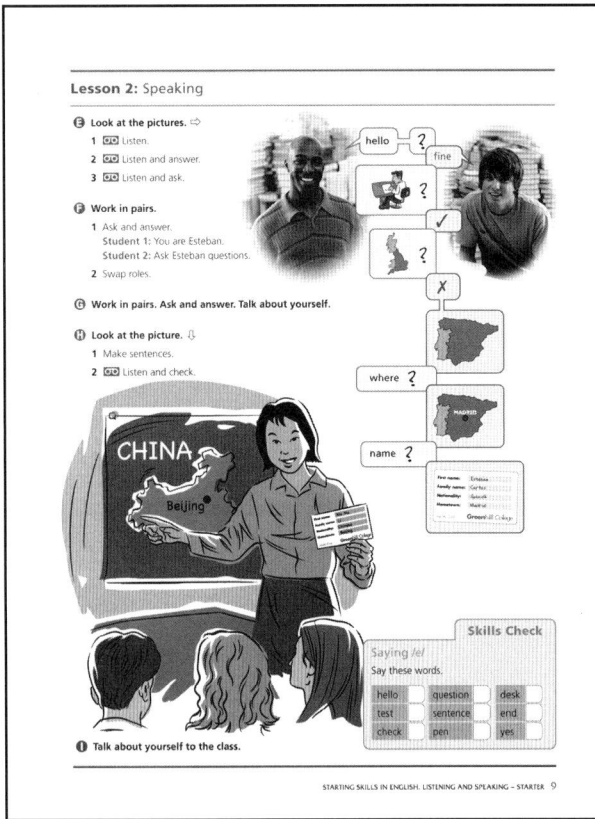

Introduction

Do some TPR which involves the key words from Lessons 1 and 2. Get students to give you instructions and follow them to the letter, i.e., do something stupid if they do not give you exactly the right instruction.

Exercise E

Refer students to the pictures. Elicit words, especially any from the theme so far which are visible. Ask students for some ideas on what the people are saying, but do not confirm or correct.

1 Set for individual work and pairwork checking. Play the tape. Pause after each exchange, i.e., question and answer, so students have time to associate the words with the prompts, but do not allow them to speak until they have heard the whole conversation.

2 Write the name of the student on the board: *Esteban Cortes*. Explain that the students must answer as Esteban. Play the tape again, pausing after each question for them to answer as Esteban, helped by the prompt. Deal with pronunciation problems as you go, focusing on the students with the biggest problems.

3 Now point out that the students must be the other person, i.e, the teacher. Play the tape again, this time pausing before each question for them to ask as the teacher, helped by the prompt. Deal with pronunciation problems as before, especially the fall-rise on *Yes / No* questions and the high start and low finish on *Wh-* questions.

Tapescript

Presenter:	Lesson 2
	E 1 Listen.
Tutor:	Hello. How are you?
Esteban:	I'm fine, thanks.
Tutor:	Are you a student?
Esteban:	Yes, I am.
Tutor:	Are you English?
Esteban:	No, I'm not. I'm Spanish.
Tutor:	Where are you from?
Esteban:	I'm from Madrid.
Tutor:	What's your name?
Esteban:	My name's Esteban. Esteban Cortes.
Presenter:	E 2 Listen and answer.
	[REPEAT OF EXERCISE E1]
Presenter:	E 3 Listen and ask.
	[REPEAT OF EXERCISE E1]

Exercise F

Put students into pairs to role-play the conversation. Make sure they swap after some time. Check individual students and correct or improve pronunciation.

Exercise G

Cross out *Esteban* (on the board) and say *Now give true information*. Check that students understand by going through the conversation with a good student. Set for pairwork. Help students, if necessary, with the English name and / or pronunciation of their nationality word and hometown. Get some students to ask you the questions. Give true information.

Exercise H

Give true information about yourself again, in the form that Xiu Xiu Li gives it in this exercise. Refer students to the second illustration.

1 Elicit what the student is probably saying. Elicit ideas, but do not confirm or correct.
2 Play the tape, pausing after each full sentence for the students to check their ideas. Elicit correct sentences.

Tapescript

Presenter: H 2 Listen and check.
Female student: My name's Xiu Xiu Li. I'm Chinese. I'm from Beijing.

Exercise I

Explain that students must now talk about themselves in the same way. Give them time to practise in pairs, then get as many students as possible to introduce themselves with the three sentences. Correct pronunciation as you go.

Skills Check

Remind students about the /e/ sound. Focus this time on the pronunciation of the sound rather than on hearing it. Point out that the letter *e* does not always make the /e/ sound. Drill the words, including those without /e/.

Language and culture note

There is no direct equivalent of /e/ in Arabic. Speakers of this language will tend to make an /i/, /æ/ or /uː/ sound instead.
There is also no direct equivalent in most Indian languages.

Closure

Ask students to tell you some more English words with the /e/ sound. Confirm or correct.

Lesson 3: Listening

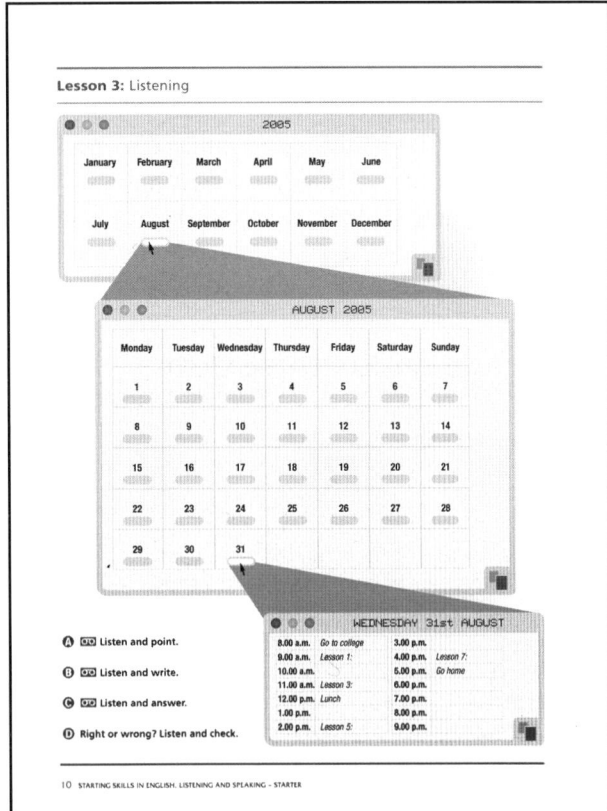

Introduction

Use some of the language from Lessons 1 and 2 to greet the students. Say some of the classroom words, and encourage students to pick up or point to each one.

Do some TPR with instructions from Lessons 1 and 2.

Write today's day, date and month on the board. See if students can tell you what the information means. Elicit ideas and explain that this is the information they will practise in Lessons 3 and 4.

Methodology notes

Avoid the temptation to turn all listening activities into speaking activities too. Although it has become tradition to follow *Listen* with *Listen and repeat*, this almost immediate transfer of focus from the receptive skill to the productive skill may not help students to become better listeners.

Speaking is much more nerve-racking in the early stage of learning than listening, and it should be possible for students to relax into the role of listeners, without worrying about the production of language. It is significant that L1 children have a long silent period, when they hear an enormous amount of language but are not expected to produce any.

Exercise A

Refer students to the first illustration – the year and the months. Say *Listen and point*. Say *A year*. If possible, walk around and check that students are pointing to the correct place. If there seem to be any problems, say *A year* again. Repeat until all the students are pointing correctly.

Repeat the procedure with *A month*.

Refer students to the second illustration. Go through the following:
a month
a year
a week
a day
a date

Refer students to the third illustration. Go through the following:
a day
a date
a month
a time

morning
afternoon
evening

Refer students back to the first illustration again. Go through the following:
the first month of the year
the last month of the year

Refer students to the second illustration again. Go through the following:
the first day of the week
the last day of the week
the first day of the month
the last day of the month
the first day of the second week
(Answer: *Monday 8*)
the last day of the third week
(Answer: *Sunday 21*)

Refer students to the third illustration again. Go through the following:
the first lesson of the day
the last lesson of the day

Indicate that the students must now find information anywhere on the page and point to it. Go through at random all the points you have covered already, or play the tape.

Tapescript

Presenter:	Lesson 3	
	A Listen and point.	
Voice 1:	a time	
	a date	
	a day	
	afternoon	
	a month	
	evening	
	a week	
	a year	
	morning	

Voice 2:	the first day of the month	
	the first day of the second week	
	the first day of the week	
	the first lesson of the day	
	the first month of the year	
Voice 1:	the last day of the month	
	the last day of the third week	
	the last day of the week	
	the last lesson of the day	
	the last month of the year	

Language and culture note

Some people in Britain and the US say that Sunday is the first day of the week, but many calendars, especially electronic ones, give Monday as the first day. It is certainly the first day of the working week in many parts of the world. Note, however, that students from some Arab countries may say that Saturday is the first day of the week, as this is the case in their countries. Thursday is often a half day, and Friday is a rest day.

Exercise B

Make a copy of the first part of the third illustration on the board, or, ideally, use an OHT. Say *Lesson 2 is at 10*. Show how this information can be added to the diary page. Do not let students write at this time. Get students to tell you where to put the information by offering to put it in the wrong place until they direct you to the correct one. Continue in the same way with the following:
Lesson 4 is at 1.
Lesson 6 is at 3.

Erase the entries from the board copy. Refer students to the third illustration again. Say *Listen and write*. Go through the same information again, or play the first part of the tape.

Tapescript

Presenter: B Listen and write.
Part 1
Voice: Lesson 2 is at 10.
Lesson 4 is at 1.
Lesson 6 is at 3.

Get students to check in pairs. Go round, if possible, and check yourself. Repeat the sentences for students who are having problems.

Refer students to your board copy or OHT. Make sure students' pens are down. Say *Lesson 1 is a test*. Show how *test* can be added to the diary entry. Continue with *Lessons 2 and 3 are English*.

Erase the entries from the board copy. Make it clear that students must now write on their diary pages. Say or play the second part of the tape.

Tapescript

Presenter: Part 2
Voice: Lesson 1 is a test.
Lessons 2 and 3 are English.

Methodology note

Students should be able to write the target words correctly if they are studying all three elements of the *Starting Skills* course.

Exercise C

Say *Listen and answer*. Make it clear that, this time, students must speak. Point out also that you are not talking about the information in the book – get students to close their books to make this clear. Ask the following questions and elicit true answers. When you have got true answers to all the questions, go back and ask the questions again at random, asking individual students, or play the tape. Do not demand full answers.

Tapescript

Presenter: C Listen and answer.
Voice 1: Is it 2006?
Is it September?
Is it Tuesday?
Is it 10 o'clock?

Voice 2: Which year is it?
Which month is it?
Which day is it?
What's the date today?
What's the time?
When's your birthday?
How old are you?

Methodology notes

1 If you allow them to, quick / garrulous students will shout out their answers before others have had a chance to even think. Prevent this by showing that they must think of an answer but not produce it until you call on them to do so. Hand signals work well for this. Point to your head (brain) and cover your lips to show thinking, then, after quite a long pause, indicate students in turn to answer. You do not have to know all the names – just use open-handed 'pointing'.

2 You may feel it is strange to ask students to answer a tape. If so, ask the questions yourself. However, there is a great advantage to students hearing questions in a variety of voices, not just yours.

Exercise D

This is the point at which you check whether individual students can do the work on the page. Go round the class and ask questions at random, or play the tape from Exercise A. Give lots of praise. Ask students to point to the following:

a year
a month
a week
a day
a time
morning
afternoon
evening
the first month of the year
the first day of the week
the first lesson of the day
the last month of the year
the last day of the week
the last day of the month
the last lesson of the day

Closure

Say to a good student: *Point to a month*. When he / she does it correctly, say *Good. You can go*. Continue, letting individual students or groups go. Stop when you think it is getting boring!

Lesson 3: Listening

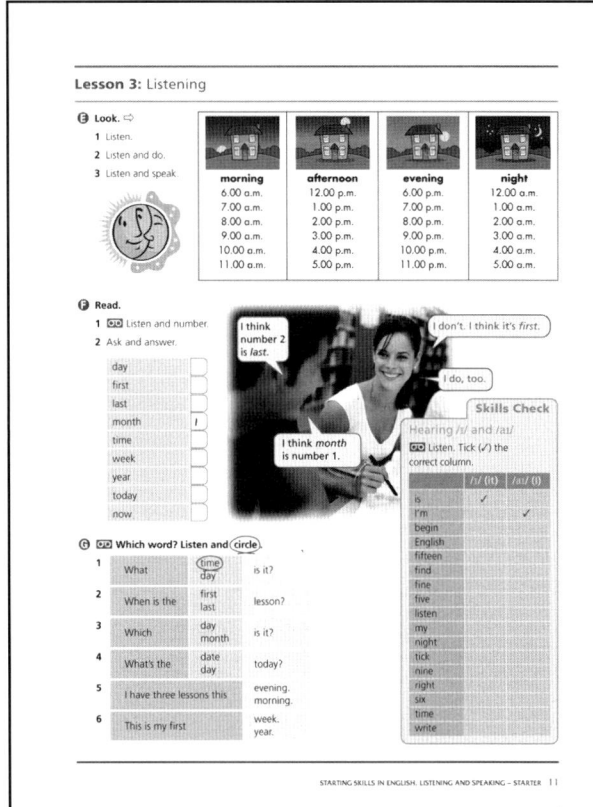

Introduction

Go through some of the words from the previous lesson, in isolation and in context, getting students to point again to the correct place on the relevant page. Ask the set of questions again and elicit replies:

Is it 2004?
Is it May?
Is it Wednesday?
Is it 3 o'clock?
Which year is it?
Which month is it?
Which day is it?
What's the date today?
What's the time?
When's your birthday?
How old are you?

Exercise E

Follow a similar procedure to that in Lessons 1 and 2. Refer students to the illustrations. Give them time to work out what they show. Say *Listen*, say each word, and do a mime to accompany it, e.g., the sun rising, the sun high in the sky, the sun setting and someone sleeping. Make sure students notice *a.m.* and *p.m.* and the points where they change. Say *morning* and students say *a.m.* Say *evening*, etc.

Reverse the activity. You say a word and the students mime it. Go faster and faster! You say *morning* and the students say *a.m.*

You say *morning* and the students say *a.m.*, etc. You say a particular time, with *a.m.* or *p.m.*, and the students say *morning*, etc.

Language and culture notes

1 The way the day is divided up into sections varies from culture to culture. At the cusp of, e.g., afternoon and evening, you may not even get people from the same culture to agree on the correct term. Is *5.00 p.m.* part of the afternoon or the evening? Is *4.00 a.m.* part of the night or the morning? This is just a schematic way of remembering the division.
2 You might like to point out that we do not use *night* with greetings, i.e., *Good night*, only with partings, which have not been revised in this course so far.

Methodology note

There is strong evidence that people learn when they are actively engaged, rather than merely passively comprehending. Words which are linked with mimes may well stick better than words which are simply processed by the brain.

Exercise F

1. Refer students to the list of words. Give them a few moments to look at the words. Do not let students speak. Say the first word, or play the tape of the first word. Show that students must write the number after the word. Continue with the second word. Set for individual work and pairwork checking. Say or play the rest of the words. Do not feedback at this point.

Tapescript

Presenter: F 1 Listen and number.
Voices:
1 month
2 first
3 time
4 year
5 day
6 last
7 today
8 now
9 week

2. This activity ensures that the students understand and can use the expressions in the speech bubbles. Refer students to the speech bubbles. Work through the mini-conversations, Teacher-Students, then half-class, then open pairs. Set for pairwork. Monitor and assist. Feed back, saying the words in order and eliciting the numbers.

Answers

day	5
first	2
last	6
month	1
time	3
week	9
year	4
today	7
now	8

Exercise G

Refer students to the first sentence. Get them to read the two alternatives: *What time is it? What day is it?* Play the first sentence. Students identify and circle the correct word. Repeat for sentence 2. Set for individual work and pairwork checking. Play the rest of the sentences, pausing after each one. Try to ensure there is complete silence so that students can process the aural trace without interference.

Feed back, just asking students for the correct word, not the whole sentence (because that puts pressure on spoken production in the middle of a listening lesson). Note that it is almost impossible to hear the difference between *day today* and *date today* because of the suppressed plosive /t/ at the end of *date*. Point out that in this case, you have to ask. Teach *day or date?*

Tapescript and answers

Presenter: G Which word? Listen and circle.
Voices:
1 What time is it?
2 When is the first lesson?
3 Which month is it?
4 What's the date today?
5 I have three lessons this evening.
6 This is my first year.

Methodology note

Knowing that you did not hear correctly is a key listening skill. Simply saying *Could you repeat that?* even in perfect English, will not get to the heart of the listening problem in such a case. Students need training in picking unusual or confusing sounds out from the stream of speech and questioning them, either to the speaker or, in a lecture situation, to a fellow student.

Skills Check

A number of words in Lessons 1 to 4 have the letter *i*, pronounced either /ɪ/ or /aɪ/. Write the example words on the board and the sound in phonemic script. Point out that you can see these signs in a dictionary. Model the sounds several times, but do not insist on the students repeating them.

Play the first word and show how you tick the first column. Repeat for the second word. Set for individual work and pairwork checking. Continue with the rest of the words. Feed back, building up the table on the board.

Tapescript

Presenter: Skills Check
Listen. Tick the correct column.
Voice: is
I'm
begin
English
fifteen
find
fine
five
listen
my
night
tick
nine
right
six
time
write

Answers

	/ɪ/ (it)	/aɪ/ (I)
is	✓	
I'm		✓
begin	✓	
English	✓	
fifteen	✓	
find		✓
fine		✓
five		✓
listen	✓	
my		✓
night		✓
tick	✓	
nine		✓
right		✓
six	✓	
time		✓
write		✓

Methodology note

It is not an aim of this course that students should become proficient in transcription into phonemic script or even reading whole words from transcription. However, with a non-phonemic language like English, i.e., one in which the sound does not always match the sight, it is extremely useful to be able to identify at least the vowel symbols and the consonant symbols where there can be confusion, e.g., /g/ and /dʒ/.

Closure

Play the *Guess the next word* game again. Say the following:
OK. Close your ... books.
That's the end of the ... lesson.
I'll see you ... (whenever is correct) at ... (whatever time is correct).
Have a nice ... (day / afternoon / evening).

Lesson 4: Speaking

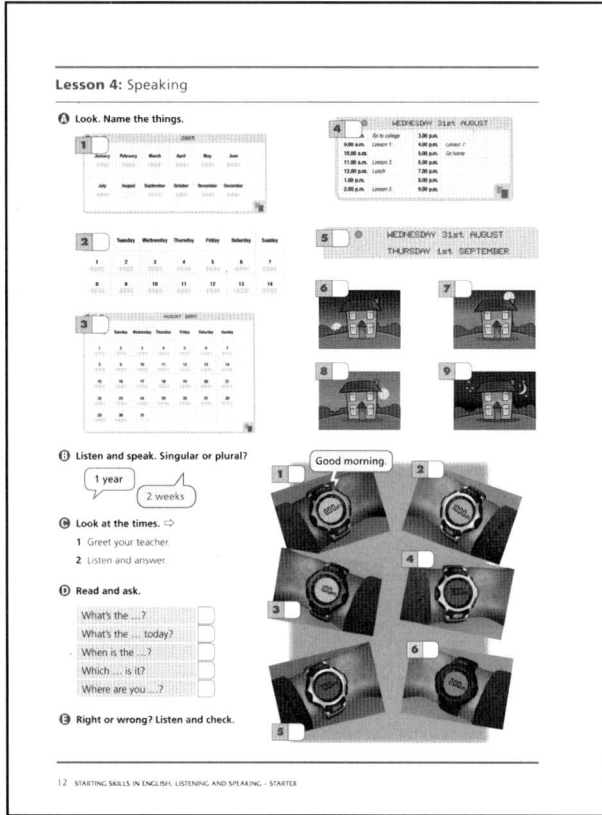

Introduction

Write the current year on the board and elicit the word *year*. Add the next few years and elicit the plural. Highlight the /z/ sound of the plural *s*. Write the current month on the board, elicit *month*, add the next few and elicit *plural*. Continue with *day* and *hour*.

Exercise A

Refer students to the illustrations. Put them in pairs to identify and say the items. Monitor and make a note of any students struggling. Give extra help now or later. Feed back, getting students to give themselves ticks if they can identify the words and say them reasonably correctly.

Methodology note

As mentioned in Lessons 1 and 2, this course focuses on general problems of phoneme production. The following are problems with this group of words which might affect some or all of your students:

Vowels
/iː/ in *week, evening*
/ʌ/ in *month*
/eɪ/ in *day, date*

Consonants
clusters: *nth* and *ft*
/d/ vs /t/
/ŋ/
not exploding any of the final plosives, i.e., in *week, month, date, afternoon, night*

Exercise B

Remind students of the two words *singular* and *plural*. Work through the words in Exercise A in order, and elicit which is which. Then say the words at random, sometimes saying the singular and sometimes the plural form. Demonstrate that there are two sounds: /s/ and /z/. Do not go into why at this time. You may find that your students cannot produce the final cluster C + *s* without putting a vowel in between the two sounds, e.g., /wiːkɪs/. Work on this but do not spend too long. The ability to produce clusters will not be taught in one lesson.

Language and culture note

Plural *s* has a /s/ sound after an unvoiced consonant, e.g., /k/.

It has a /z/ sound after a vowel or a voiced consonant, e.g., /eɪ/; /n/.

Exercise C

Draw a digital watch face on the board and mark the time – the hour closest to the current time. Point to the time, then say, as appropriate, *Good morning, Good afternoon* or *Good evening*.

1   Refer students to the illustrations and show how the time should prompt the greeting. Say *1*. Elicit *Good morning*. Continue with the other prompts.
2   Say times at random and elicit the appropriate greeting. Improve pronunciation, chorally and individually.

Exercise D

Write the word *time* on the board followed by a question mark. Elicit the question. Continue with the other prompts. Confirm or correct, then drill with back-chaining, e.g.,
> *date?*
> *date today?*
> *the date today?*
> *What's?*
> *What's the date today?*

At the end, get students to ask the questions and you give truthful answers. Put students into pairs to ask and answer.

Exercise E

Go through the whole page once more, encouraging students to give themselves a tick for each activity they can do successfully. Tell students to work on the ones they got wrong in their own time.

Closure

Point to singular or plural items in the classroom and elicit the correct word. If there are problems with final clusters, spend a few more moments on correcting and improving.

Lesson 4: Speaking

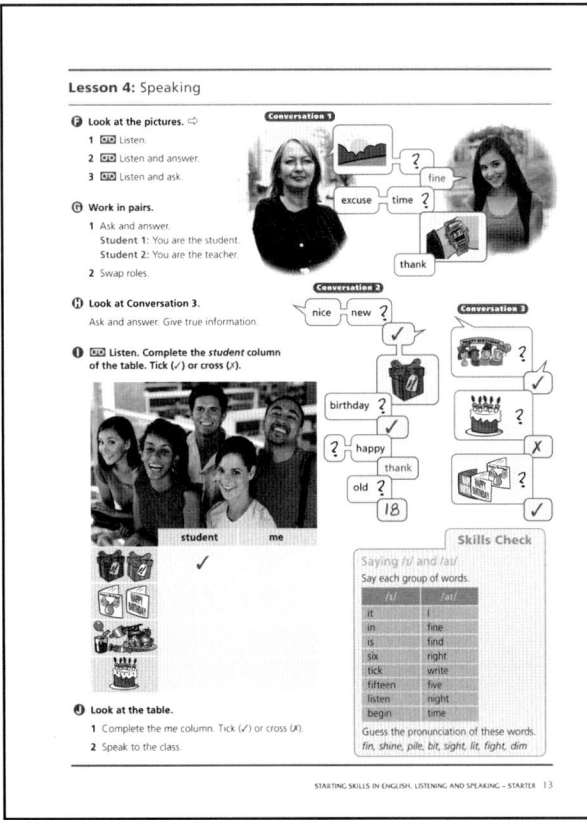

Introduction

Ask the year, month, day, date and time (if it is near a whole hour). Say *one year, two ...*, and elicit the plural form. Repeat for other items from Lessons 1–4.

Exercise F

Refer students to the pictures. Elicit words, especially any from the lessons to date. Ask students for some ideas on what the people are saying, but do not confirm or correct.

1 Set for individual work and pairwork checking. Play the tape. Pause after each exchange, i.e., question and answer, so students have time to associate the word with the prompts, but do not allow them to speak until they have heard the whole conversation.

2 Write *Student* on the board and explain that students must answer as the student. Play the tape again, pausing after each question for them to answer, helped by the prompt. Deal with pronunciation problems as you go, focusing on students with the biggest problems.

3 Write *Teacher* on the board and repeat the procedure with students acting as the teacher.

Tapescript

Presenter: Lesson 4
F 1 Listen.
Conversation 1
Teacher: Good morning. How are you?
Student: I'm fine, thanks.
Teacher: Excuse me. What's the time?
Student: It's 8.
Teacher: Thank you.

Presenter: Conversation 2
Teacher: That's nice. Is it new?
Student: Yes, it is. It's a birthday present.
Teacher: Oh, is it your birthday today?
Student: Yes, it is.
Teacher: Really? Happy birthday.
Student: Thank you.
Teacher: How old are you?
Student: I'm 18.

Presenter: Conversation 3
Teacher: Do you have a birthday party in your country?
Student: Yes, we do.
Teacher: Do you have a birthday cake?
Student: No, we don't.
Teacher: What about cards ... birthday cards?
Student: Yes, we do. We have birthday cards.

Presenter: F 2 Listen and answer.
[REPEAT OF EXERCISE F1]

Presenter: F 3 Listen and ask.
[REPEAT OF EXERCISE F1]

Exercise G

Put students into pairs to role-play the conversation. Make sure they swap after some time. Check individual students and correct or improve pronunciation.

Answers

birthday presents	✓
birthday cards	✓
party	✗
birthday cake	✗

Exercise H

Refer students specifically to the third conversation. Elicit the form of the questions and short answers with *do*. Drill the questions and short answers with *do*. Drill the sentences with *have* and *don't have*. Make sure students are approximating to *don't* with a diphthong /əʊ/, rather than a short /ɒ/ sound.

Put students in pairs to ask and give true answers.

> **Methodology note**
>
> This kind of exercise obviously works better if there is a real information gap. If you do have students from different cultures in your class, make sure you address the questions to a range of students. Make sure also that students are working in pairs and groups with individuals from different cultures.

Exercise I

Refer students to the picture above the table. Demonstrate that they must listen and tick or cross the points (*presents*, etc.). Set for individual work and pairwork checking. Play the tape. Feed back, building up the table on the board.

Tapescript

Presenter: I Listen. Complete the *student* column of the table. Tick or cross.

Student: In my country, we have birthday presents. We have birthday cards. We don't have a party. We don't have a birthday cake.

Exercise J

Add the third column to the table on the board. If you are from a different culture to the students, add ticks and crosses which are true for you.

1 Set for individual work.
2 Help students to make the four sentences with *have* and / or *don't have*. If students are from different cultures, get a few of them to give their talks. If they are all from the same culture, go round and listen to as many students as possible individually.

Skills Check

Remind students about the /ɪ/ and /aɪ/ sounds. Focus this time on the pronunciation. Show how the /ɪ/ sound requires spread lips while the /aɪ/ sound starts with a more open mouth and moves to /ɪ/. Drill the words in each set, building up the table on the board. Then elicit specific words from different students by pointing to them on the board.

Closure

Ask students to tell you some more English words with the sound /ɪ/. Confirm or correct. Possible words at this level are *sit, him, his, thin, sing, this*.

Repeat with /aɪ/. Possible words at this level are *light, mine, white, high*, plus *my, try, buy* which don't fit either pattern here.

RECURRENT THEME STRUCTURE

Lesson 1 is a test or deep-end-strategy lesson on listening in a particular theme area. Remember! This is a book for false beginners, not true beginners. It is expected that students will get between 90% and 100% of the items at the beginning of every Lesson 1 right. Make this clear to students. Say, e.g., *You know this*. OR *This is not new*. OR *You did this in X year*. OR *Let's check these words*. It is absolutely essential that all students realise this is revision and that you do not think this is new learning. Not only does this raise motivation – to show what they know. It also removes any fear that you are looking for something more complex, something they have never done.

Lesson 2 highlights and does remedial work on the listening points in Lesson 1. There is also some speaking in this lesson of words and sentences that have been highlighted to date.

Lesson 3 is a test or deep-end-strategy lesson on speaking in a particular theme area. The purpose is the same as Lesson 1. As with Lesson 1, it is expected that students will get between 90% and 100% of the items at the beginning of this lesson right. Make this clear to students. Make a note of students who get specific items wrong and try to ensure they are getting those items right by the end of Lesson 4.

Lesson 4 highlights and does remedial work on the speaking points in Lesson 3.

THEME 1 Work and Business

General note
By the end of this theme, students should be able to hear and identify, in isolation and in context, the following words linked with work and business. They should also be able to say them with reasonable pronunciation and use them in simple S V O sentences.

accountant	hotel	secretary
bank	job	start (*v*)
computer	lawyer	teacher
court	office	want
doctor	receptionist	work (*v*)
hospital	school	

In addition, students should also be able to hear and say:
- a number of jobs
- some places of work
- numbers with a tens item and a unit, e.g., *24*.

In fact, it is assumed that these false-beginner students will be reasonably confident with these items, although they may still have problems with pronunciation and spelling.

Lesson 1: Listening

Introduction

Use some of the language from Starter Lessons 1 and 2 to greet the students.

Check classroom language. Say some of the classroom words, and encourage students to pick up or point to each item. Check plural *s* as you go by sometimes saying, e.g., *desks*. Check that students point to more than one object.

Do some TPR with instructions from Starter Lessons 1 and 2.

Elicit the day, the date and the month. Ask about birthdays.

Exercise A

Follow a similar procedure to that in Starter Lessons 1 and 2. Refer students to the illustration. Say or play the first part of the tape, with the words in isolation. Students point to the correct person shown on the poster.

Tapescript

Presenter:	Theme 1 Work and Business
	Lesson 1
	A Listen and point.
	Part 1
Voice:	accountant
	doctor
	engineer
	lawyer
	receptionist
	secretary
	teacher
	typist

Say or play the second part of the tape, with the words in context. Students point to the correct person. Monitor and note students who are having difficulties.

Tapescript

Presenter:	Part 2
Voice 1:	Are you a typist?
Voice 2:	Where's the doctor?
Voice 1:	I want to see a lawyer.
Voice 2:	This is Miss Smith, your new teacher.
Voice 1:	I work in an office. I'm a secretary.
Voice 2:	Do you want to be an accountant?
Voice 1:	I want to be a computer engineer.
Voice 2:	I work at Greenhill College. I'm a receptionist.

Exercise B

Say one of the job names and do a mime. Make it funny, but most importantly, make it memorable. Remember your visual learners! When you have done all the jobs and mimes, say a job and encourage the students to do the related mime.

Exercise C

Ask a student: *Are you a typist?* Elicit *No (I'm not)*. Show that it is more polite to say *No, I'm not*. You can do this by saying *No* in a very brusque way. Ask a few more students about some of the other jobs.

Ask a student: *Do you want to be a typist?* Elicit *Yes / No (I don't)*. Stress the word *want* and show that it relates to the future. Repeat the point about the rudeness of the monosyllable. Ask a few more students about some of the other jobs.

Ask the two questions at random, checking on students' ability to reply appropriately with *I'm not / I do / don't*.

Exercise D

Go round the class, repeating the various points, or play the tape from Exercise A. Get students to give themselves ticks for getting the jobs right, and praise them for doing mimes and answering questions appropriately.

Closure

Help individual students who struggled during the lesson and allow them to leave when they can get most of the points correct immediately.

Lesson 2: Listening

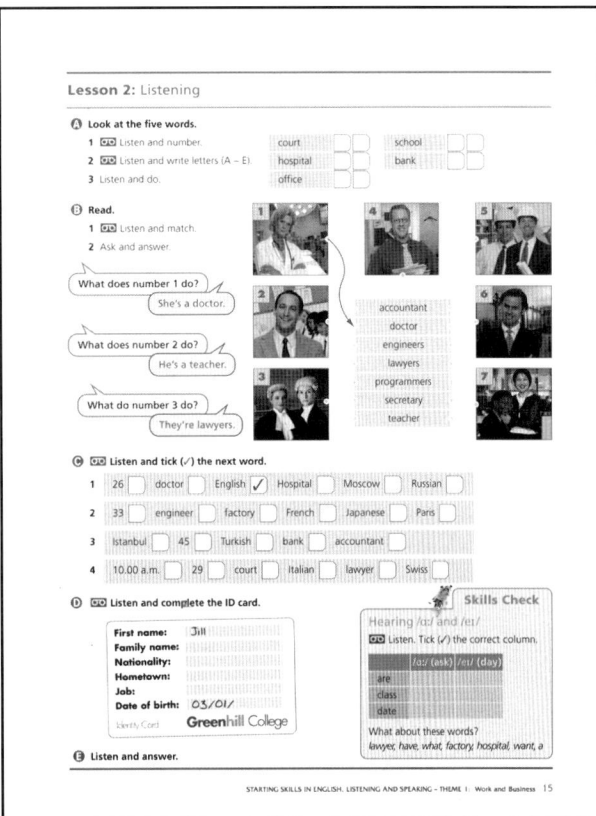

Introduction

Go through some of the words from Lesson 1, in isolation and context, getting students to point again to the correct place on the relevant page. Ask the two types of questions again, at natural speed:

Are you a / an ...?
Do you want to be a / an ...?

Exercise A

1 Refer students to the five words in the list. Say or play the tape of the words in isolation. Students number the words in the first column. Feed back by saying the words and getting students to shout out the number.

Tapescript

Presenter:	Lesson 2
	A 1 Listen and number.
Voice 1:	1 school
	2 office
	3 court
	4 hospital
	5 bank

2 Refer students to the second column. Explain, or mime, that this time they are going to hear each word in a sentence. They must write a letter *A*, *B*, *C* or *D* beside the word. Say or play the tape of the words in context.

Tapescript

Presenter:	A 2 Listen and write letters A to E.
Voice 2:	A Where do you go to school?
	B Is there a hospital near here?
	C Do you work in an office?
	D What time does the court start?
	E When does the bank open?

Answers

court	3	D
hospital	4	B
office	2	C
school	1	A
bank	5	E

3 Refer students to the big picture on page 14 again. Say each word in isolation from the list and students have to point. Use the mime again, this time for the place rather than the person. Remind students of the mimes, then say each word and get students to do the appropriate mime.

Exercise B

Play the first exchange. Show students how to match with the arrow. Set for individual work and pairwork checking. Play the other exchanges, pausing after each one to allow students to match.

Tapescript

Presenter:	B 1 Listen and match.	
	1	
Interviewer:	What do you do?	
Female voice:	I'm a doctor.	
Presenter:	2	
Interviewer:	And you, sir. What do you do?	
Male voice:	I'm a teacher. I work at Greenhill College.	
Presenter:	3	
Interviewer:	Excuse me. What do you do?	
Female voice 1:	We're lawyers.	
Female voice 2:	Sorry, we're late for court.	
Presenter:	4	
Interviewer:	Sir, could you tell me your job?	
Male voice:	I'm a secretary.	
Presenter:	5	
Interviewer:	What do you do?	
Male voice 1:	We're engineers.	
Interviewer:	Are you computer engineers?	
Male voice 2:	No, we work in a factory.	
Presenter:	6	
Interviewer:	Are you an accountant?	
Male voice:	Yes, I am. I work in this bank.	
Presenter:	7	
Interviewer:	What do you two do?	
Female voice 1:	We're programmers.	
Female voice 2:	Yeah. Programmers.	

Answers

2 teacher
3 lawyers
4 secretary
5 engineers
6 accountant
7 programmers

Ask the questions in the speech bubbles to feed back on Exercise 1. Then work through the three conversations, building them up on the board and highlighting the agreement points: *does she / he + he's / she's a ...*, then *do they + they're ...s*. Set for pairwork, but do not worry too much about the pronunciation at this point.

Methodology notes

1 As mentioned before, this is *reading* in a *listening* lesson, because of the importance of making sound-sight relationships in a language that is not phonemic.
2 This is *speaking* in a *listening* lesson. It is a good way to fix language that you have heard.

Exercise C

Remind students of the importance of predicting the next word. Give some examples of how you can do this, e.g., say *My name is ...* (assuming they know your name!). *You are in class ... This lesson ends at ...,* or other suitable sentence openers.

Refer students to the first set of words. Play the first text. Show how you can predict the next word. Get students to say the word on this occasion to demonstrate comprehension of the activity as well as the sentence. Set for individual work. Play the rest of the texts.

Play all the texts again, getting students to say the next item at each pause.

Tapescript

Presenter: C Listen and tick the next word.
1
Voice: Elena Markova lives in England, but she isn't [PAUSE] English. She's [PAUSE] Russian. She's from [PAUSE] Moscow. She's [PAUSE] 26. She's a [PAUSE] doctor. She

                  works in Greenhill [PAUSE] Hospital.

Presenter: 2
Voice: Pierre Auguste lives in Japan, but he isn't [PAUSE] Japanese. He's [PAUSE] French. He's from [PAUSE] Paris. He's [PAUSE] 33. He's an [PAUSE] engineer. He works in a car [PAUSE] factory.

Presenter: 3
Voice: Bulent Okan is [PAUSE] Turkish. He's [PAUSE] 45. He's from Ankara, but he now lives in [PAUSE] Istanbul. He's an [PAUSE] accountant. He works in a large [PAUSE] bank.

Presenter: 4
Voice: Paola Franchetti lives in Switzerland, but she isn't [PAUSE] Swiss. She's [PAUSE] Italian. She's a [PAUSE] lawyer. She's [PAUSE] 29. It's [PAUSE] 10.00 and she's in [PAUSE] court.

Exercise D

Remind students that it is important to listen for information like names and numbers, and not to worry about the whole sentence.

Refer them to the ID card. Elicit examples of each type of information. Ask them also what information is missing from the Date of birth section (It's the year). Set for individual work and pairwork checking. Play the tape.

Students will probably not be able to complete the Date of birth section on their own. Elicit that Jill is 23; therefore, students take 23 years away from the year they are in. This will give them the correct year. Elicit the whole of her birth date, i.e., *The third of January, 19…*

Highlight the expression *come from*. Until now, the students have learnt *be from*, i.e., *She's from London* vs *She comes from London*. Point out that they mean the same.

Tapescript

Presenter: D Listen and complete the ID card.
Voice: Jill Cast works at Greenhill Bank. She is British. She lives in Greenhill now but she comes from London. She works in the computer department. She's a computer programmer. She's 23.

Answers

First name:	Jill
Family name:	Cast
Nationality:	British
Hometown:	London
Job:	computer programmer
Date of birth:	03/01/…*

* This depends on when the course is taught.

> **Methodology note**
>
> There is a fair amount of irrelevant information in this short text. This is deliberate. Listening for information to meet an established need is a key listening skill.

Exercise E

Refer students to the ID card again. Ask *What's her first name?* to elicit the first piece of information. Students can give short answers, as they might in real life. Move on to the other questions. Ask the questions more quickly and at random. Ask for the same information in different ways, putting slightly extra stress than normal on the key word or words, e.g.,

Could you tell me her first name? Do you know her family name? Is she British, by the way? Where's she from, I mean, where does she come from originally? Put students in pairs to try to ask and answer about Jill.

Closure

Refer students to the Skills Check. Highlight the two letter names as examples of the vowel sounds. Say or play the words for students to identify. Feed back, building up the table on the board. Elicit some other words for each group, e.g.,

/ɑː/ (ask)	/eɪ/ (day)
car	came
star	make
farm	eight
part	play
fast	stay

Answers

	/ɑː/ (ask)	/eɪ/ (day)	
are	✓		words with *a* + *r* often = /ɑː/
class	✓		words with *a* + *s* often = /ɑː/
date		✓	words with *a* + C + *e* often = /eɪ/

Ask about the words underneath. Point out that they all have the letter *a* but they don't make either of the target sounds.

Tapescript

Presenter: Skills Check
Listen. Tick the correct column.
Voice: are
class
date

Lesson 3: Speaking

Feed back, getting students to give themselves ticks if they can identify the words and say them reasonably correctly.

Start to use the red S during this exercise to highlight the plural s.

Methodology note

Some or all of your students might have problems with the following pronunciation points:

Vowels
/ə/ at the end of all the words except *secretary*
/aɪ/ in *typist*
/ɔɪ/ in *lawyers*
silent letter in *secretary*

Consonants
clusters: *cr, ct, gr, ng, nt, pr, pti, st*

Stress
a*ccoun*tant
engin*eers*
rec*ep*tionist

Introduction

Remind students of the plural *s* by showing them singular items and plural items and getting them to repeat accurately, then pointing to singular and plural items for them to produce the appropriate form.

Write a large red *S* on an A4 sheet of paper and stick it on the wall – if that is allowed – in a specific location. (If you are not allowed to put things on the wall, write the *S* in a particular place on the board, e.g., top left.) For the rest of the lesson, every time students make a mistake with the plural *s*, point to the red *S*.

Exercise A

Refer students to the illustrations. Set for pairwork. Make a note of any students struggling. When students are getting the noun correct, get them to make full sentences with contractions. Give help now or later.

Exercise B

1 Play the first extract without introducing it. Then say *Where are we?* Elicit ideas, then confirm. Put students into pairs to work out and feed back on the rest of the extracts in turn.
2 Play the first extract again. Ask *Who works here?* Elicit the target word(s), then any other words that the students know. Confirm.

Possible answers

Exercise B1	Exercise B2
office	typist
classroom	teacher
court	lawyer
office	secretary
factory	engineer
office	accountant
hospital	doctor
office	programmer
office (hotel)	receptionist

Tapescript

Presenter: Lesson 3
B 1 Listen. Identify the sounds.

Sound effects:
1 typewriter
2 classroom noises
3 courtroom noises
4 someone dictating a letter
5 factory noises
6 accounting machine and mumbling of numbers
7 hospital noises
8 computer noises
9 noises from the reception area of an office

Presenter: B 2 Listen again. Who works here?
[REPEAT OF EXERCISE B1]

Exercise C

Tell students you are thinking of a job – from the ones on page 16. They can ask *Do you ...?* and they can guess with *Are you ...?* Do this once or twice as an example. Allow other well-formed and appropriate questions, e.g., *Do you work inside?*

Drill the questions.

Set for pairwork. Monitor and assist.

Exercise D

Write the first question in full on the board. Highlight the key words. Elicit, with pens down, the other questions. Get students to ask you the questions and give truthful replies (except *How old?* if you don't want to tell students your age).

Drill the questions.

Set for pairwork. Monitor and assist.

Closure

Say the stressed sounds from the list of jobs. Get students to tell you the full word, e.g., You say *pro*, the students say *programmer*.

Methodology note

This activity helps with listening and speaking. On the one hand, because native speakers tend to only make stressed syllables salient, other vowels change to /ə/, other consonants are swallowed. Therefore, as a listener to English, students must be able to identify words from their stressed syllable. Conversely, students must stress the right part of a word, otherwise native speakers will not identify the word correctly.

Lesson 4: Speaking

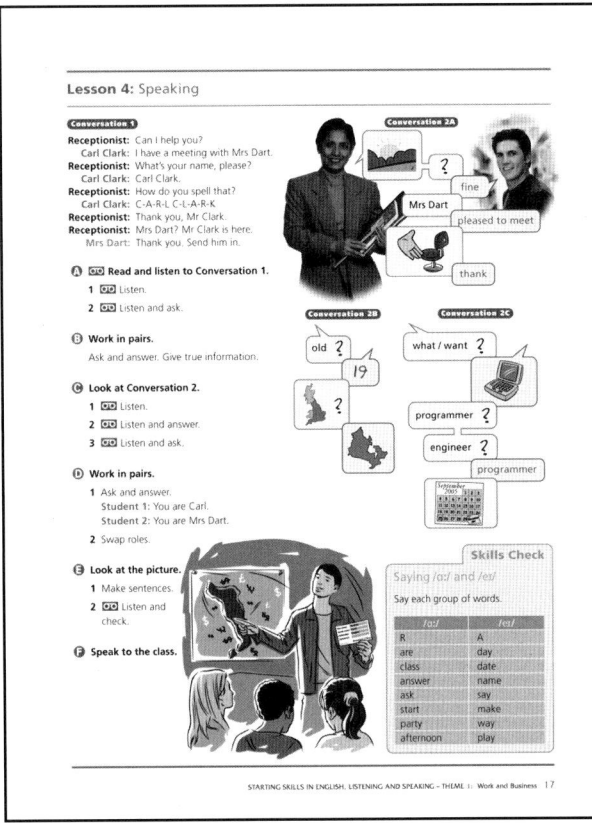

Introduction

Mime some jobs from this theme and get students to say the name. Put students into pairs, if you wish, to play the game.

Exercise A

Ask students to cover the texts on this page and look only at the first picture. Ask them what the receptionist is saying and what the man is saying. Elicit, but do not confirm or correct.

1 Play Conversation 1.
2 Play Conversation 1 again, pausing after the receptionist's questions to get the replies, then play each reply for students to check.

Tapescript

Presenter:	Lesson 4
	A 1 Listen.
Receptionist:	Can I help you?
Carl:	I have a meeting with Mrs Dart.
Receptionist:	What's your name, please?
Carl:	Carl Clark.
Receptionist:	How do you spell that?
Carl:	C-A-R-L C-L-A-R-K
Receptionist:	Thank you, Mr Clark.
	Mrs Dart? Mr Clark is here.
Mrs Dart:	Thank you. Send him in.
Presenter:	A 2 Listen and ask.
	[REPEAT OF EXERCISE A1]

Exercise B

Let students read Conversation 1. Build up the receptionist's questions on the board as follows:

Receptionist:	Can I help you?
Carl:	
Receptionist:	What's your name, please?
Carl:	
Receptionist:	How do you spell that?
Carl:	
Receptionist:	Thank you, Mr Clark.

Drill the questions, especially the new ones.

Get students to ask you the questions and give true answers. They must write down your name, with the correct spelling. Then get them to dictate it back to you. Set for pairwork. Monitor and assist, especially with the names of letters.

Exercise C

1. Set for individual work. Students listen to Conversation 2, following in their books. Pause the tape a few times, if necessary, to give students time to associate words and prompts, e.g., *morning* = *Good morning*.
2. Tell students to take the part of Carl. Play the tape, pausing each time after Mrs Dart's words for students to respond as Carl.
3. Repeat the procedure with students taking the part of Mrs Dart. Deal with pronunciation problems, chorally and individually.

Tapescript

Presenter:	C 1 Listen.
Mrs Dart:	Good morning, Mr Clark. How are you?
Carl:	I'm fine, thanks.
Mrs Dart:	I'm Mrs Dart.
Carl:	I'm pleased to meet you.
Mrs Dart:	Come in. Sit down.
Carl:	Thank you.
Mrs Dart:	How old are you, Carl?
Carl:	I'm 19.
Mrs Dart:	Are you English?
Carl:	No, I'm Canadian.
Mrs Dart:	So, what do you want to do?
Carl:	I want to work with computers.
Mrs Dart:	Do you want to be a programmer? Or do you want to be an engineer?
Carl:	A programmer, I think.
Mrs Dart:	Well, the classes start on September 25th …
Presenter:	C 2 Listen and answer. [REPEAT OF EXERCISE C1]
Presenter:	C 3 Listen and ask. [REPEAT OF EXERCISE C1]

Exercise D

Set for pairwork. Monitor and assist.

Exercise E

Refer students to the illustration at the bottom of page 17. Elicit possible sentences, e.g., *He's Italian. / He's from Milan.* See if students can think of other things to say about him, e.g., age, occupation, planned occupation.

Play the tape. Ask questions about the student. *What's his name?* etc.

Tapescript

Presenter:	E 2 Listen and check.
Andrea:	My name is Andrea Totti. I'm Italian. I'm 20. I'm at Greenhill College. I want to work with numbers. I want to be an accountant.

Exercise F

Explain that students must give the same information about themselves as Andrea. Give them some time to work out what to say, then set for pairwork. Monitor. Choose a few students to give their talks in front of the class.

Closure

Work through the Skills Check. Drill the sounds. Show that the /ɑː/ sound is more rounded than the /eɪ/ sound. Show also that the diphthong has two sounds, similar to /e/ + /iː/.

Get students to see or remember the patterns here:
/ɑː/ often = *ar, as*
/eɪ/ often = *a + C + e; ay*

THEME 2 Science and Nature

General note
By the end of this theme, students should be able to hear and identify, in isolation and in context, the following words linked with nature and colour. They should also be able to say them with reasonable pronunciation and use them in S V C sentences where C is an adjective (colour or temperature), e.g., *The sky is blue.*

Nature	Colour
cloud	black
cold	blue
grass	brown
hot	colour (*n*)
sand	green
sky	grey
snow	orange
sun	red
tree	white
	yellow

For the purposes of talking about the rainbow, etc., other colour words will be used. These are not target words.

Lesson 1: Listening

Introduction

Refer students to the illustrations on pages 6, 10 and 14. Revise all the vocabulary, for both listening and speaking.

Exercise A

Refer students to the illustration. Follow the usual procedure.

Play the tape of words in isolation, then in context.

Monitor and note students who are having difficulties.

Tapescript

Presenter: Theme 2 Science and Nature
Lesson 1
A Listen and point.
Voice: sky
clouds
sun
trees
snow
sand
grass
mountain

The sky is blue.
The clouds are black.
The snow is cold.
What colour are the trees?
The sun is hot today.
The sand is orange.
The grass is green.

Methodology note

Give the name of the object going across the sky, if asked. It is a *rainbow*. You can also give the name of the set of colours, if asked. It is the *spectrum*.

Exercise B

Pick up or point to objects with each of the target colours. Then play the tape. As usual, students point while you monitor and note students who are having difficulties. There are at least two things with the target colour in each case. Say the colours again in isolation, at random, getting faster and faster.

Tapescript

Presenter: B Listen and find.
Voice: Find something yellow.
Find something orange.
Find something white.
Find something black.

Find something green.
Find something brown.
Find something blue.
Find something grey.
Find something red.

> **Methodology note**
>
> Do not worry about pronunciation at this point. Students can even point to a colour if they want to.

Exercise C

Ask the questions or play the tape. As this is a listening lesson, one-word answers are fine.

Tapescript

Presenter:	C Listen and answer.
Voice:	What colour is the snow?
	What colour is the sun?
	What colour is the sky?
	What colour is the sand?
	What colour are the trees?
	What colour are the clouds?
	What colour are the mountains?

Exercise D

Follow the usual procedure to check individual success at the various tasks in this lesson.

Closure

Tell students: *My favourite colour is ...* Make clear the meaning of *favourite*. Also say *I hate ...* Mime, if necessary.

Ask:
> *What's your favourite colour?*
> *Which colour do you hate?*

Help individual students who struggled during the lesson and allow them to leave when they can get most of the points correct immediately.

Lesson 2: Listening

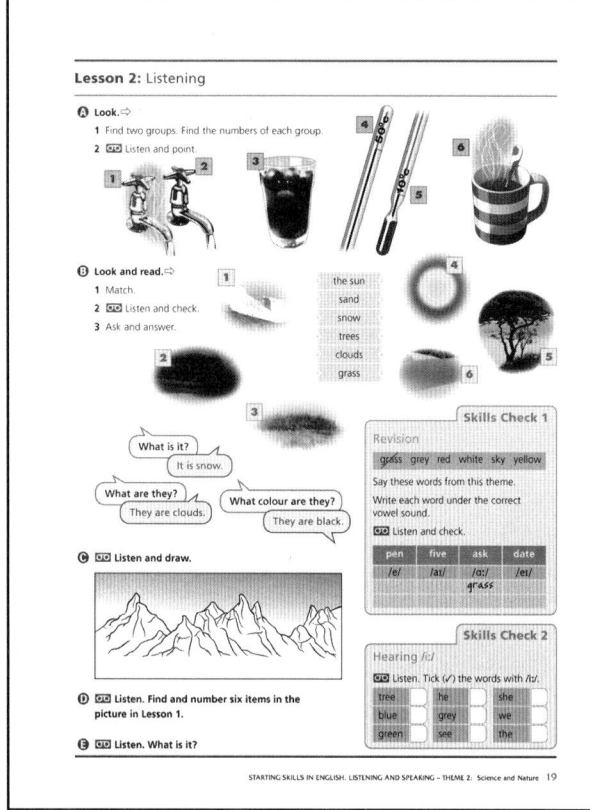

Answers
Group 1
Picture 2 – cold-water tap (cold)
Picture 3 – cola with ice cubes (very, very cold)
Picture 5 – thermometer showing a low temperature (very cold)

Group 2
Picture 1 – hot-water tap (hot)
Picture 4 – thermometer showing a high temperature (very hot)
Picture 6 – cup of coffee (very, very hot)

Tapescript
Presenter: Lesson 2
A 2 Listen and point.
Voice: It's cold.
It's hot.
It's very cold.
It's very, very hot.
It's very hot.
It's very, very cold.

Introduction

Go through some of the words from Lesson 1, in isolation and context, getting students to point appropriately.

Ask questions with the form *What colour is / are …?*

Exercise A

Refer students to the illustrations.

1 Give the instruction. Set for pairwork. Elicit some answers, but do not confirm or correct.
2 Say or play the tape.

Mime being cold. Say *cold*. Mime being hot. Say *hot*. Then refer students to the illustrations again and say:
Find something cold. (snow)
Find something hot. (sand, sun)

Exercise B

1 Set for individual work and pairwork checking. Do not confirm or correct.
2 Play the tape. Feed back, eliciting the correct match for each word. Drill the questions and the answers. Point out the agreement elements. Students should be able to make the contractions now for *What's, It's, They're*.
3 Set for pairwork.

Answers
1 snow
2 clouds
3 grass
4 the sun
5 trees
6 sand

Tapescript

Presenter: B 2 Listen and check.
1
Voices: What is it?
It is snow.
What colour is it?
It is white.

Presenter: 2
Voices: What are they?
They are clouds.
What colour are they?
They are black.

Presenter: 3
Voices: What is it?
It is grass.
What colour is it?
It is green.

Presenter: 4
Voices: What is it?
It is the sun.
What colour is it?
It is yellow.

Presenter: 5
Voices: What are they?
They are trees.
What colour are they?
They are brown.

Presenter: 6
Voices: What is it?
It is sand.
What colour is it?
It is orange.

Language and culture note

This small group of nouns contains several problems. At this stage it is best to just teach the noun phrases as fixed expressions. Do not go into the reasons.

snow, grass, sand – uncountable, so *is*
cloud, tree – countable, so *are*
sun – only one, so *the*

Exercise C

Draw a mountain horizon on the board. Say to a student: *Draw the sun in the sky*. Give him / her the marker and see if he / she does it correctly. Continue until someone does it correctly. Say *Draw a cloud in the sky*. Choose another student to try and draw it. Refer students to the mountain horizon in their books. Set for individual work and pairwork checking. Get students to cover their own work while they listen. Play the tape.

Feed back, playing the tape again and getting students to come up and complete a new mountain horizon on the board.

Tapescript

Presenter: C Listen and draw.
Voice: Look at the picture.
You can see some mountains.
Draw the sun in the sky.
Draw four clouds in the sky.
One cloud is white. Two clouds are grey. One cloud is black.
Draw some snow on the mountains.
Draw some grass and some trees.

Exercise D

Say or play the first one as an example. Then set for teacher-paced pairwork, i.e., say or play the description, pausing after it. Give a few moments for pairs to discuss their ideas, then play the next part for the answer. Feed back, eliciting what was said on the tape.

Answers

A 1 the sun
G 2 the sky
D 3 clouds
B 4 sand
E 5 grass
F 6 trees

Tapescript

Presenter: D Listen. Find and number six of the items in the picture in Lesson 1.
Voice: 1 It is very, very, very hot. In the morning and the evening it is red. During the day it is yellow or orange. [PAUSE] It is the sun.
2 At night it is black. In the morning it is grey and then blue. [PAUSE] It's the sky.
3 Sometimes they are white, sometimes they are black, sometimes they are grey. [PAUSE] They are clouds.
4 It is sometimes yellow or orange. In some places, it is red. In other places, it is white. You find it in hot places. [PAUSE] It is sand.
5 It is usually green, but when it is very hot and very dry it is brown. [PAUSE] It is grass.
6 In cold months they are brown. In hot months they are brown and green. Sometimes they have red or yellow or blue or orange parts. [PAUSE] They are trees.

Exercise E

Explain that this is the same kind of exercise as D. Say or play the tape, pausing as before. Do not play or say the ending until you have given the students plenty of time to say what the object is and check with a partner. Feed back, referring them to the colours from the rainbow in Lesson 1.

Tapescript

Presenter: E Listen. What is it?
Voice: It is in the sky when there are clouds and the sun is shining. It is red, orange, yellow, green, blue, indigo and violet. [PAUSE] It is a rainbow.

Closure

Work through the Skills Checks.

Skills Check 1

Remind students of the sounds of the example words from Starter and Theme 1. Isolate the vowel sound.

1 Give students time to say the words to themselves.
2 Ask them to write the words in the spaces.
3 Play the tape. Feed back, building up the table on the board. Say the words or play the tape several times, but do not insist on students repeating. Remember that this lesson focuses mainly on listening. Point out some common sound-sight relationships, as shown in the answers.

Answers

	pen /e/	five /aɪ/	ask /ɑː/	date /eɪ/
word(s) from this theme	*red* *yellow*	*white* *sky*	*grass*	*grey*
sound-sight patterns	*e* often = /e/	final C + y often = /aɪ/ (*try, my, fly,* cf *grey*) i + C + e often = /aɪ/ (*fine, time, ice*)	a + s / ss often = /ɑː/ (*last, fast, pass*)	final V + y often = /eɪ/

Tapescript

Presenter: Skills Check 1
Listen and check.
Voice: grass
grey
red
white
sky
yellow

Skills Check 2

Follow the usual procedure. Point out that *ee* in the middle of a word or *e* at the end often make the /iː/ sound. Elicit more words with the sound /iː/ (*thirty, thirteen,* etc.).

Answers

tree	✓
blue	
green	✓
he	✓
grey	
see	✓
she	✓
we	✓
the	✓

Tapescript

Presenter: Skills Check 2
Listen. Tick the words with /iː/.
Voice: tree
blue
green
he
grey
see
she
we
the

Methodology note

Strictly speaking, the sound of *y* after a consonant at the end of a word, e.g., *thirty*, is not the long vowel /iː/. However, it is not the short vowel /ɪ/ either! The sound is closer to the long vowel than the short and can be taught as the same.

Lesson 3: Speaking

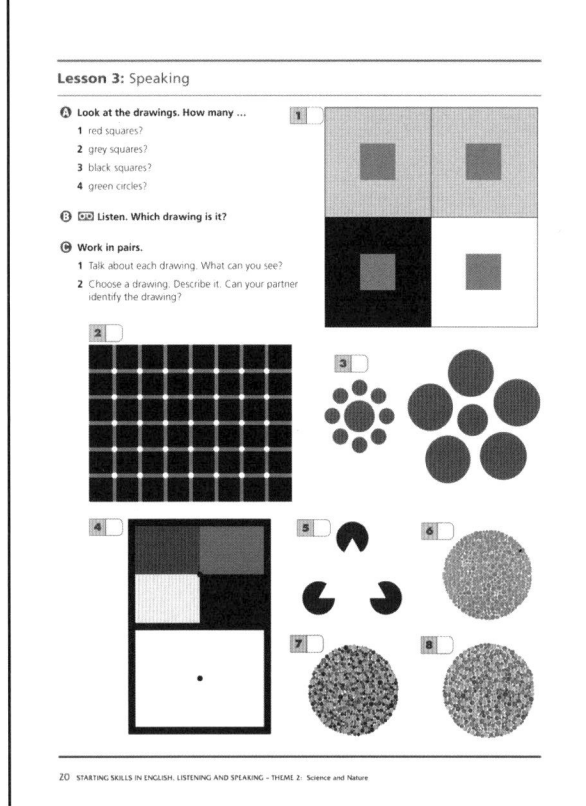

Show some pictures of broad landscapes with several of the target items in and ask:
>   *Can you see ...?*

Elicit / Teach *Yes, I can. / No, I can't.* Make sure students are distinguishing clearly between the two vowels, i.e., /kæn/ vs /kɑːnt/.

After some time, move on to *What can you see?*

Allow students to give just nouns first, then nouns and colour adjectives, e.g., *Trees ... they're brown.* Then model the target sentence, e.g., *I can see brown trees.*

Ask students about the classroom, i.e., *What can you see in this classroom?* Elicit sentences with the same pattern.

Language and culture note

The most salient difference between the positive modal *can* and the negative *can't* in writing is the apostrophe *t*. It is reasonably clear that this form is negative as it looks similar to *aren't* and *don't*, etc. However, in speech, there is a much more salient difference – vowel length. It is probable that native-speaker listeners identify the sentence as negative from the vowel length, rather than from the /t/ sound on the end, which may, in any case, be elided with the following consonant (e.g., in *I can't type; I can't drive*) or even change to another consonant (e.g., unexploded /m/ in *I can't believe*).

Exercise A

Refer students to the drawings. Draw a square on the board and elicit / teach *square*. Draw a circle on the board and elicit *circle*. Set for pairwork. Elicit ideas. Feed back, pointing out the correct number in each case.

Introduction

Take in pictures of key natural items from Lessons 1 and 2, i.e.,
>   clouds: different colours
>   the sun: different colours
>   the sky: different colours
>   snow: falling and lying
>   sand: different colours
>   trees: with various coloured flowers and fruit on
>   grass: different colours

Flash these pictures and elicit the names and the colours, asking:
>   *What is it? What are they?*
>   *What colour is it? What colour are they?*

Deal with pronunciation problems.

Answers
1. red squares = 1
2. grey squares = 6 (4 small squares and 2 larger ones in Drawing 1)
3. black squares = 49 (1 in Drawing 1 and 48 in Drawing 2)
4. green circles = 15

Exercise B

Tell students they are going to hear descriptions of the drawings. They must identify the correct drawing in each case.

Set for individual work and pairwork checking. Play the first description as an example.

Elicit ideas, then confirm. Play the remainder of the items. Feed back. Note that the final three drawings are not described in this activity.

Highlight extra vocabulary points as follows:
light / dark + colour
small / large + *square / circle*

Highlight new patterns as follows:
There is / are …
It has / They have …

Answers
A   Picture 2
B   Picture 1
C   Picture 5
D   Picture 3
E   Picture 4

Tapescript

Presenter:	Lesson 3	
	B Listen. Which drawing is it?	
	A	
Voice:	The drawing has lots of squares. They are all black. It has grey lines between the black squares. It has white circles at the corners of the squares.	
Presenter:	B	
Voice:	The drawing has four squares. Each square has another square in the middle. Two large squares are grey, one is black and one is white. All the small squares are grey.	
Presenter:	C	
Voice:	There are three circles. They are brown. The circles have a small section missing.	
Presenter:	D	
Voice:	The drawing has two main circles. There are other circles around these two main circles. The circles around one circle are small. The circles around the other circle are large.	
Presenter:	E	
Voice:	The drawing has two squares. One square has coloured squares – red, light blue, violet and yellow. One square is white. There is a black circle in the middle of each square.	

Exercise C

1. Refer students to the first drawing. Elicit a description with *I can see* ... Turn some of the sentences into *There is / are* ... or *It has / They have* ...
2. Demonstrate how the activity works, perhaps doing an open-pair activity with two good students. Set for pairwork. Monitor and assist. Feed back, dealing with any items that arise, and particularly with the correct pronunciation of colour words.

Methodology note

This is a deep-end strategy activity to see how well students can use language from the descriptions in Exercise A and / or remember previously learnt items to help with the activity.

Closure

Point out that there is something strange about each one of the drawings. Ask students to look at them before the next lesson and try to work out what is strange – and how to explain it in English.

Lesson 4: Speaking

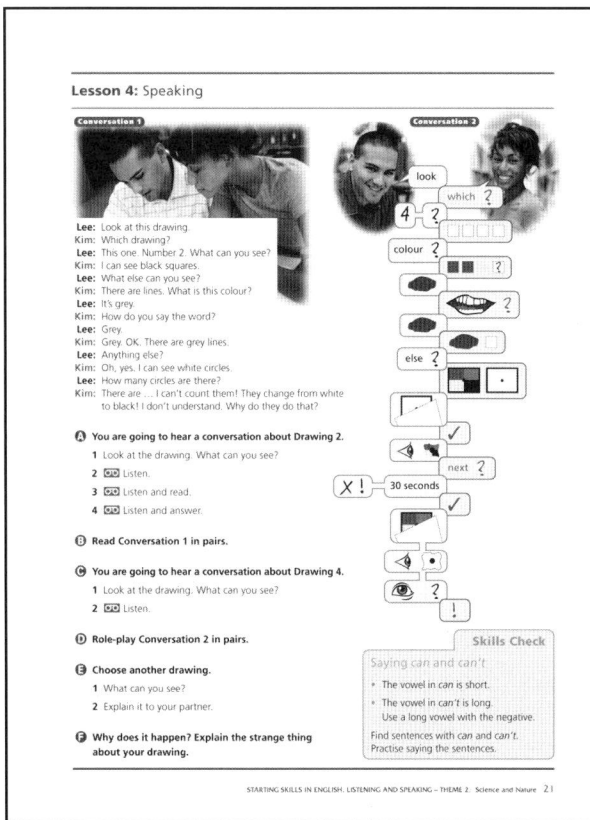

Introduction

Refer students to the drawings in Lesson 3 again. Ask students what is strange about the drawings. Elicit some ideas, with students using their available language. Encourage contributions if students have things to say, but do not confirm or correct with regard to the strangeness. However, if students make mistakes with the target vocabulary or structure (*There is ... / It has ... / I can see ...*), do correct.

Exercise A

1 Refer students to Drawing B. Ask students: *What can you see?* Elicit some sentences. Do not confirm or correct.

2 Tell students to cover Conversation 1. Play the first conversation. Pause at [PAUSE] for students to find the section that is being described.

Tapescript

Presenter: Lesson 4
A 2 Listen.
Conversation 1

Lee: Look at this drawing.
Kim: Which drawing?
Lee: This one. Number 2. What can you see?
Kim: I can see black squares.
[PAUSE]
Lee: What else can you see?
Kim: There are lines. What is this colour?
Lee: It's grey.
Kim: How do you say the word?
Lee: Grey.
Kim: Grey. OK. There are grey lines.
[PAUSE]
Lee: Anything else?
Kim: Oh, yes. I can see white circles.
Lee: How many circles are there?
Kim: There are ... I can't count them! They change from white to black! I don't understand. Why do they do that?

3 Allow students to look at Conversation 1. Play the tape. Pause a few times for students to associate sound and sight.

Tapescript

Presenter: A 3 Listen and read.
[REPEAT OF EXERCISE A2]

4 Tell students to cover the conversation again. Ask Kim's main questions or play the tape, and elicit replies, i.e., *What can you see? What else can you see? Anything else?* Drill the questions.

Tapescript

Presenter: A 4 Listen and answer.
[REPEAT OF EXERCISE A2]

Refer students to the final part of the conversation. Repeat Kim's final section. Highlight the final question: *Why do they do that?* Elicit some ideas. If students are struggling, allow them (if feasible) to discuss the point in their own language.

Otherwise, just say and mime:
You look at white. You can see white. You look at white in another place. You can see black. Your brain sees the opposite colour – white to black.

Highlight the key exchange over pronunciation. Write it on the board, i.e.,
 Lee: *It's grey.*
 Kim: *How do you say the word?*
 Lee: *Grey.*
 Kim: *Grey.*

Point out that Kim repeats the word to check pronunciation. Practise the exchange with other colour words, e.g., you initiate by saying *It's red / black / blue*, etc.

Methodology note

Reading and listening at the same time is not a cheat! Associating the sound and sight of words and sentences is a vital part of learning to listen and learning to speak.

Exercise B

Set for pairwork. Monitor and assist. Work particularly on pronunciation of the target structures and vocabulary.

Exercise C

Follow the normal procedure for this kind of activity. Play Conversation 2 then elicit sentences from the prompts.

Tell students to follow the procedure. Then say *What can you see?*

Students should see the 'opposite' colours when they look at the white square. Ask *Why does it happen?* and elicit / tell / mime that it is the same effect as the black and white circles in Drawing 2.

Tapescript
Presenter:	C 2 Listen.
	Conversation 2
Teenage boy:	Look at this drawing.
Teenage girl:	Which drawing?
Teenage boy:	This one. Number 4. What can you see?
Teenage girl:	I can see four squares.
Teenage boy:	What colour are they?
Teenage girl:	One square is red, one is blue, one is yellow and … what colour is that?
Teenage boy:	It's violet.
Teenage girl:	How do you say the word?
Teenage boy:	Violet.
Teenage girl:	Violet. OK. And one square is white. [PAUSE]
Teenage boy:	What else can you see?
Teenage girl:	There is a black circle in the middle of the coloured squares and there's a black circle in the middle of the white square.
Teenage boy:	OK. Cover the white square.
Teenage girl:	Yes.
Teenage boy:	Look at the black circle in the middle of the coloured squares.
Teenage girl:	OK. What next?
Teenage boy:	No! Look for 30 seconds.
Teenage girl:	Right.
Teenage boy:	OK. Now cover the coloured squares. Look at the black circle in

	the middle of the white square. What can you see? [PAUSE]
Teenage girl:	I can see … Oh! I can see colours. I can see four coloured squares. Blue, orange, or red, yellow and … What is the name of the colour?
Teenage boy:	Violet.
Teenage girl:	That's amazing! Why does that happen?

Exercise D

Set for pairwork. Monitor and assist. Work on individual pronunciation.

Exercise E

Set for pairwork. Monitor and assist.

Exercise F

This could be done in the students' own language, if feasible. Otherwise, elicit some ideas, with students using their available language.

Answers

drawing	effect	cause
1	The central grey squares are different colours.	They are actually the same colour, but the surrounding colour makes the eye see something different.
2	The white circles change to black.	The eye sees the opposite colour when you look away.
3	The central circle on the left is bigger than the one on the right.	They are actually the same size; the eye sees the left one as bigger because it is inside small circles, and vice versa.
4	The eye sees coloured squares, not the white square.	The eye sees the opposite colour when you look away.
5	The eye sees a triangle.	There is not a triangle – the eye fills in shapes that are not there. **Note:** You will need to teach / elicit the word *triangle*.
6, 7, 8	These are colour blindness tests; there is the number 12 in 6, the number 26 in 7 and a wiggly route in 8.	If students cannot see the number, they could have slight colour blindness.

Closure

Work through the Skills Check. Point out the two vowel sounds and drill them in isolation and in context. Ask students to just say *positive* or *negative* when you say sentences, e.g.,

        You say: *I can see four colours.*
Students say: *Positive.*
        You say: *I can't see the number.*
Students say: *Negative.*

Make any sentences with *can* and *can't*. Don't restrict yourself to sentences from this theme, or even the use of *can* for possibility. Sentences like *I can't type* are also good as tests of the ability to hear the longer vowel and hence the negative.

THEME 3: The Physical World

General note

By the end of this theme, students should be able to hear and identify, in isolation and in context, the following words linked with the physical world. They should also be able to say them with reasonable pronunciation and use them in simple S V O A sentences, where S = *There*, V = *is / are*, O = noun and A = prepositional phrase, e.g., *There are mountains in the north*.

bottom	mountain
centre	north
city	right
coast	river
country	south
east	top
island	town
lake	village
left	west
map	

Lesson 1: Listening

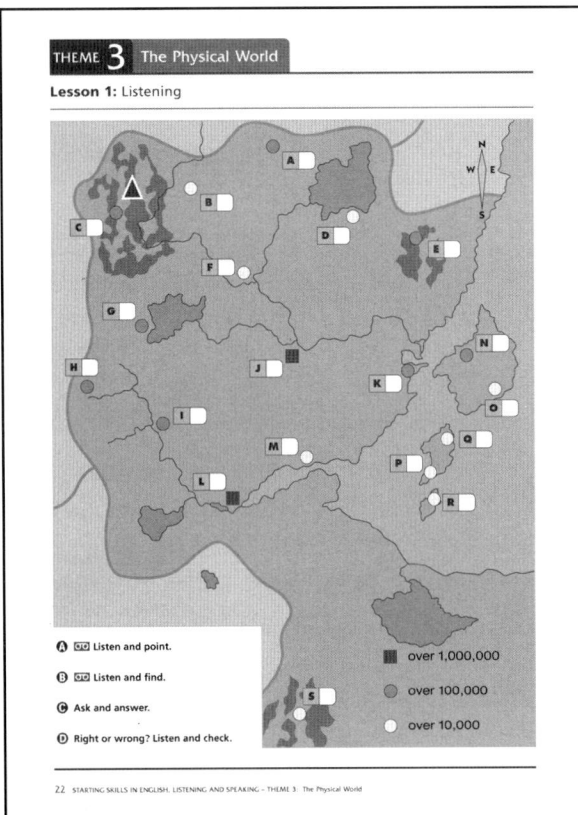

Introduction

Tell the students 10 things about yourself, using language from the Starter and the first two themes, e.g.,

1 *My first name is Alan.*
2 *My family name is Dent.*
3 *I'm Canadian.*
4 *I'm from Toronto.*
5 *I'm 32.*
6 *I'm a language teacher.*
7 *I can speak French and Spanish.*
8 *My birthday is 23rd March.*
9 *I live in a flat.*
10 *My bedroom is green.*

Ask students to tell each other 10 things about themselves.

Methodology note

It may not be obvious to students that each theme has enabled them to say something extra about themselves. This exercise should reinforce this point.

Exercise A

Draw the legend symbols on the board. Elicit the names of each, i.e.,

  red square orange circle yellow circle

Give the meaning of each, i.e., *city*, *town* and *village*. Show the size relationship and give examples from the students' own culture, or the area you are giving the lesson in, e.g., *Beijing is a city*.

Refer students to the map. Ask *What can you see?* Elicit some ideas. Confirm any correct points. Teach / Elicit *map*.

Say or play the first half of the tape with the words in isolation. Students point to the part of the picture. Note that in this case there is more than one correct place in several instances, e.g., *city*. Pause the tape after each item and say *Anywhere else?*

Say or play the second half of the tape with the words in context. Students point to the correct part of the picture. In this case, there is only one correct place.

Tapescript

Presenter: Theme 3 The Physical World
     Lesson 1
     A Listen and point.
Voice: city
   town
   village
   island
   lake
   mountain
   river
   coast
   north

south
east
west
centre
northeast
southwest
northwest
southeast

There are mountains in the northwest.
There is a lake in the southeast.
There is a large island.
There is a town in the north.
There are mountains in the south.
There is a city on the coast.
There is a city on a river.
There is a village on a lake.
There is a town in the centre.

Exercise B

Tell the students: *Listen to these people. Where does each person live? Write the number next to the place.*

Answers
1   K
2   F
3   R
4   S
5   E

Tapescript

Presenter: B Listen and find.
Voices:
1 I live in a town. It is on the coast.
2 I live in a village. It is on two rivers.
3 I live on an island. It is a very small island. There is only one village.
4 I live in a town. It is in the south of the country. I don't live on the coast. I live in the mountains.
5 I live in a town in the east of the country. It is in the mountains.

Exercise C

Tell students to work in pairs. Each pair must choose a place to live in Polonia, then listen and answer questions about it. They can only answer *Yes* or *No* with the appropriate ending, e.g., *Yes, we do. / No, it isn't.*

Work through an example with a good pair. Say the questions. Establish first whether the place is a village, town or city, then which part of the country it is in. The other students must listen to the answers and guess at any time. If they are right, repeat with another pair. If they are wrong, continue until the place is pinpointed.

Possible questions
Do you live in a village / a town / a city?
Is it in the north / south / east / west of the country?
Is it in the mountains / on an island / on the coast / on a river / on a lake?

Try to get through at least five pairs.

Repeat the activity with each student working on his / her own. Try to get round at least 10 individuals.

Exercise D

Go round the class, repeating the various points and getting students to give themselves ticks for getting the places right, and praising for answering questions appropriately.

Closure

Help individual students who struggled during the lesson and allow them to leave when they can get most of the points correct immediately.

Lesson 2: Listening

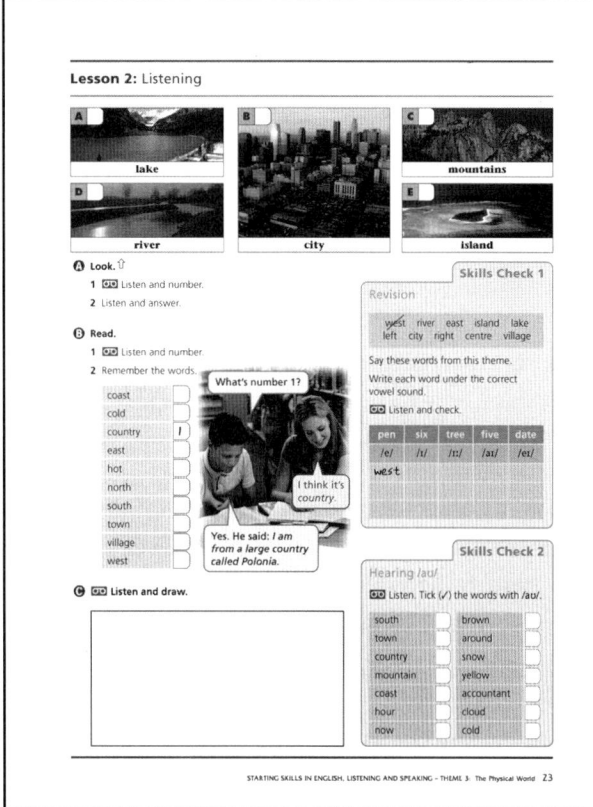

Introduction

Make sure students can understand the four main points of the compass. Say and write on the board the first letters: N, S, E, W – and the four secondary points – say and add NE, NW, SE, SW. Make sure students can also understand the idea of *centre*. Write C at the centre of the compass.

Go through some of the words from Lesson 1, in isolation and context, getting students to point again to the correct place on the relevant page. Elicit the correct letter for different places as follows:

> You say: *It's a town in the south of the country. It's in the mountains.*
> Students say: *It's S.*

Also ask questions with *How many X are there in Polonia?*

Encourage students to count in English as they are working it out. Get them to answer with *There are* + number.

Draw a compass indicator on the board – the kind that appears on the map in Lesson 1.

Exercise A

1   Refer students to the four pictures. Set for individual work and pairwork checking. Play the tape. Students number the pictures. Feed back.
2   Refer students to the pictures again. Say *The lake and the river are on the left. The mountains and the island are on the ...* . Try to elicit *right*. Otherwise, teach the word. Ask *Where are the lake and the river?* Elicit *On the left*. Repeat for *mountains* and *island*. Repeat the procedure with *top* and *bottom*. Ask students: *Where is the lake?* Try to elicit *It's top left*. Repeat for the other items. Point out that we can use *centre* in this situation too – *The city is in the centre*. Build up a diagram on the board for sets of pictures as for points of the compass with TL, TR, etc.

Answers
A 2
B 5
C 1
D 4
E 3

Tapescript
Presenter: Lesson 2
 A 1 Listen and number.
Voices: 1 My house is high up in the mountains.
 2 I live in a small house on a lake.
 3 I come from a tiny village on an island.
 4 There is a small river in my town.
 5 I come from the capital city of my country.

Exercise B

1. Give students time to look at the words and think about the sounds. Set for individual work and pairwork checking. Play the tape. Do not pause on this occasion, unless students are really struggling. The aim is for students to pick out a word from the stream of speech and then be ready for the next one along. Clearly, the target words are key words from the text.
2. In the pairwork checking, ask students to remember what the speaker said, e.g.,

    1 country. He said: I am from a large country called Polonia.

    Feed back, eliciting the answer and the memory of the exact sentence in each case.

Answers

coast	5
cold	6
country	1
east	4
hot	7
north	
south	
town	3
village	2
west	

Methodology note

This exercise is not an introduction to reported speech. There is no change of pronoun – *I* to *he* – and no backshifting – e.g., *He said he was ...* The introductory expression *He said* can be taught as a phrase. The aim is for students to use a key word to reconstruct the actual words spoken, from aural memory and knowledge of English sentence patterns.

Tapescript

Target words in italics

Presenter: B 1 Listen and number.
Man: I am from a large *country* called Polonia. I come from a *village*. Well, no, it's not a village really. It's a small *town*. It is in the *east*. It isn't near the *coast*. It's high up in the mountains. It's very *cold* in December and January, but it's *hot* in June and July.

Exercise C

Explain that students are going to hear about another person. Refer them to the map of Borland. Set for individual work and pairwork checking. Play the tape, ideally all the way through, but pause after the key points if students are struggling.

Feed back, getting students to complete a copy on the board.

Model answer

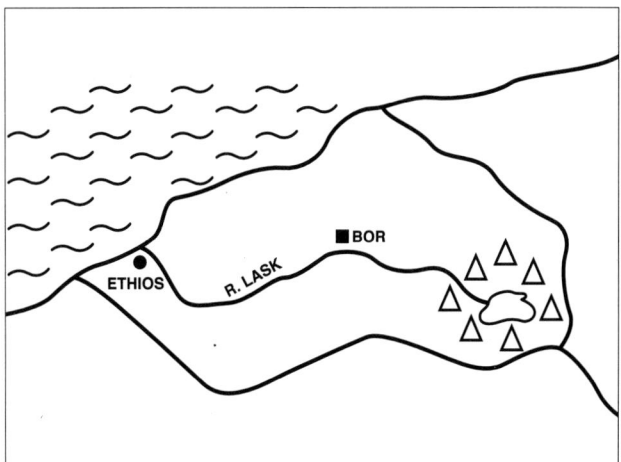

Tapescript

Presenter: C Listen and draw.
Woman: I come from a small country called Borland. The capital city is in the centre of the country. It is called Bor – B-O-R. But I come from the west of the country. My town is on the coast. It is called Ethios – E-T-H-I-O-S. It's very hot in August but it's quite cold in February. My town is on a river. It is the river LASK – L-A-S-K. The river comes from a lake. The lake is in the mountains in the southeast of the country. Bor, the capital, is on the river Lask, too.

Closure

Refer students to revision Skills Check 1. Check the pronunciation of the example words.

1 Elicit the words from the students and correct the pronunciation of the (stressed) vowel sound.
2 Give students time to try to place the words in the correct column.
3 Say or play the words for students to identify. Feed back, building up the table on the board. Elicit some other words for each group.

Answers

pen	six	tree	five	date
/e/	/ɪ/	/iː/	/aɪ/	/eɪ/
west	river	east	island	lake
left	city	right		
centre	village			

Tapescript

Presenter: Skills Check 1
Listen and check.
Voice: west
river
east
island
lake
left
city
right
centre
village

Refer students to Skills Check 2. Model the target sound. Play the tape.

Feed back, building up the table on the board. Ask students if they can see any patterns.

Answers

south	✓
town	✓
country	
mountain	✓
coast	
hour	✓
now	✓
brown	✓
around	✓
snow	
yellow	
accountant	✓
cloud	✓
cold	

Possible patterns:
ou and *ow* sometimes = target sound, but cf *country, snow, yellow*

Tapescript

Presenter: Skills Check 2
Listen. Tick the words with /aʊ/.

Voice: south
town
country
mountain
coast
hour
now
brown
around
snow
yellow
accountant
cloud
cold

Lesson 3: Speaking

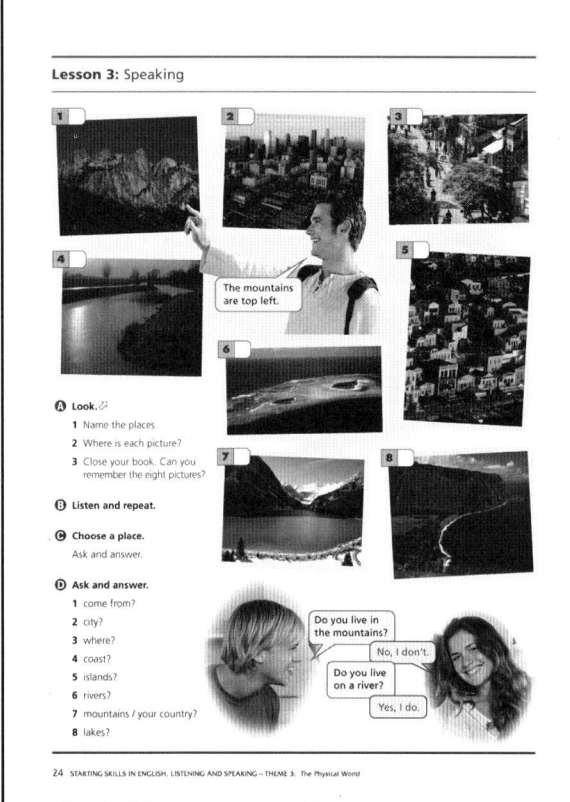

Introduction

Draw a horizontal line on the board. Elicit *line*. Add a vertical line. Elicit *cross*. Point to the top of the vertical line. Elicit *north*. Repeat for all the other main points.

Add a smaller saltire cross on top of the other. Point to one of the points and elicit, e.g., *northeast*. Repeat for all the other points.

Ask some general questions that require the use or understanding of these points of the compass, e.g.,
> Give me the name of a city in the northeast of your country.
> Where are we at the moment? (e.g., *in the southeast of the UK*)

Exercise A

1. Refer students to the pictures. Set for pairwork. Make a note of any students who are struggling. Give help now or later. Feed back, getting students to give themselves ticks if they can identify the words and say them reasonably correctly.
2. Remind students about *top left*, etc. Set for pairwork. Note that they will need to 'invent' expressions such as *top centre*, *left centre* to accommodate all the pictures. Feed back with the two questions *Where is / are the X? What's top left?* etc.
3. Set for pairwork, with students testing each other. Feed back, getting the whole class to try to remember the set of pictures.

Methodology note

Check that students are stressing the first syllable of the two-syllable words. Do not let them get away with full vowels on the unstressed syllables in the following words:
> *mountains* – unstressed vowel reduced to /ɪ/
> *village* – unstressed vowel reduced to /ɪ/
> *island* – unstressed vowel reduced to /ə/
> *river* – unstressed vowel reduced to /ə/

Make sure also that they are saying the clusters with reasonable accuracy, as follows:
> *mountains* – /nt/ and /nz/
> *islands* – /ndz/
> *coast* – /st/

Exercise B

Refer students to the top-left picture and say *I live in the mountains*. Get students to repeat the phrase *in the mountains*. Refer students to the centre-left picture and say *I live on a river*. Get students to repeat *on a river*. Continue with all the other pictures. Build up a table on the board as follows:

in	a town
	a village
	a city
	the mountains
on	a river
	a lake
	an island
	the coast

Highlight the special points relating to *a / an / the*. Do not attempt to explain these points, just teach them as fixed phrases.

Language and culture notes

1. We say *on a river / lake* when we actually mean *beside a river / lake*. Make sure students realise this. *On an island* is more obvious, but *on the coast* perhaps also means *beside* rather than literally *on*.
2. We say *in <u>the</u> mountains*, perhaps because the noun is plural.

Exercise C

Tell students you live in one of the places in the pictures. Elicit a question. If students are struggling, refer them to the speech bubbles. Drill the questions. Change the nouns and check that students can make the whole questions correctly, e.g.,

You say: *Mountains.*
Students say: *Do you live in the mountains?*

You say: *River.*
Students say: *Do you live on a river?*

Set for pairwork. Monitor and confirm or correct.

Exercise D

Work through the prompts, eliciting possible questions. When you have a good question, drill it.
Point out that you can ask about countries in two main ways:

Do you have (e.g., *mountains in your country)?*

or

Are there any (e.g., *mountains in your country)?*

Drill both questions.

Point out that we often use *What about (mountains)?* so we don't have to repeat the question exactly.

Set for pairwork. Monitor and confirm or correct.

Answers
Possible questions
Target elements in italics

1. *Where do you come from?*
2. *Do you live in a city?*
3. *Where is it?*
4. *Is it on the coast?*
5. *Are there many islands?*
6. *What about rivers?*
7. *Do you have mountains in your country?*
8. *Are there any lakes?*

Closure

Refer students to other pages of the course with a range of pictures. Elicit where each picture is, e.g., *top left*.

Lesson 4: Speaking

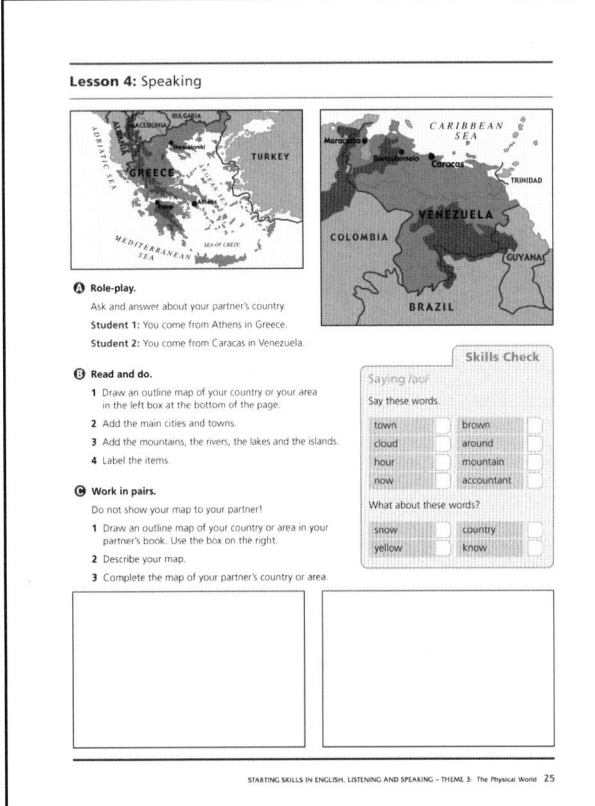

Introduction

Take in a map of the world. Point out the country you are in. Get students to tell you countries that are north, south, east and west of this country. Ask about specific countries and elicit whether they are north, etc.

Point out the countries of Greece and Venezuela. Explain that you are going to talk about these countries in this lesson.

Work out the direction to each country from the students' own country and, if different, from the place where they are studying.

Ask questions about physical features in the two countries, e.g.,
> Are there any mountains in Greece? What about Venezuela? etc.

Exercise A

Put students into pairs. Tell each pair to look at the relevant map and work out where the capital is, where the other main cities are, and where the target physical features are – the mountains, rivers, lakes and islands.

Go round and help each pair.

Leave students in their pairs to role-play the conversation. Monitor and assist. Choose one or two pairs to perform in front of the class.

Exercise B

Draw an outline map of your country on the board to show that anyone can do it! Follow the instructions in the course book, talking about your country as you go, using the target language, e.g.,
> I come from ...
> The capital is ...
> It is in the centre of the country / on the coast / on a river.
> There are mountains in the southwest of the country. They are called ...

Use the symbols from Lesson 1 for *city*, *town*, *mountains*, etc.

Set for individual work. Teach or elicit the word *label*, i.e., add names. Monitor and assist, especially with the names of places in English where they are different from the names in the students' own language.

Methodology notes

1. If students all come from the same country, encourage them to draw a map of their province / state or of a different country that they know well. Then for Exercise C, put them in pairs from different provinces / states / countries.
2. If you are able to display students' work in your classroom, consider giving out pieces of paper for students to draw their outline maps on, and display these at the end of the lesson.

Exercise C

Erase the details of your country from the board. Dictate the information again and get students to come up and add information and label it.

Set for pairwork. Monitor.

Closure

Work through the Skills Check.

THEME 4: Culture and Civilization

General note
By the end of this theme, students should be able to hear and identify, in isolation and in context, the following words linked with people. They should also be able to say them with reasonable pronunciation and use them in simple S V O A sentences, e.g., *You can drive a car at 16.*

adult	man / men
boy	old
child / children	person / people
female	teenager
friend	woman / women
girl	young
male	

Lesson 1: Listening

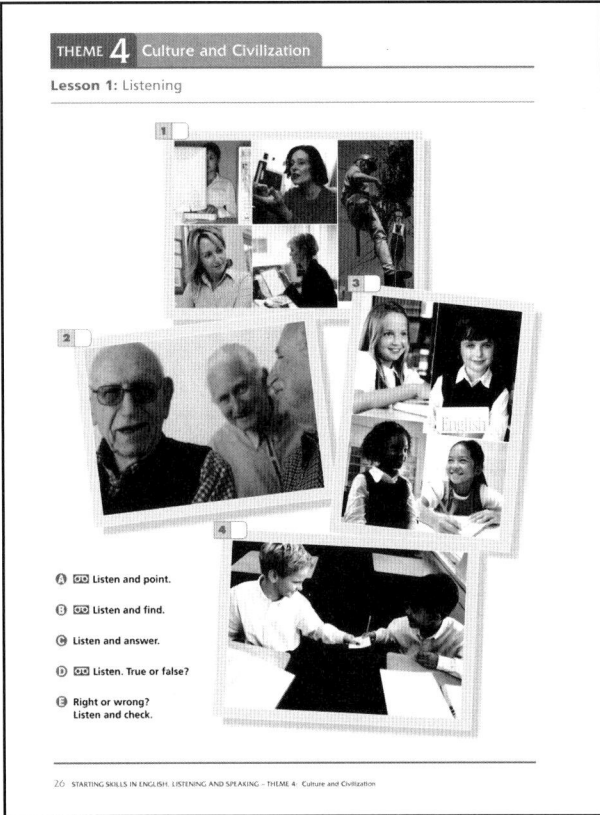

Introduction

Refer students to the pictures. Focus on items in the pictures from previous themes, including colours, e.g., *Find a desk, chair, telephone. Can you see the colour red?* etc.

Ask *What can you see on the left / right / at the top / at the bottom?* Elicit answers, but do not confirm or correct.

Exercise A

Say *OK. Let's check these words*. Say or play the tape with the words in isolation. Students point to the part of the picture. Note that for the first set of words, there is more than one correct place. Pause the tape after each item and say *Anywhere else?* Continue until all examples have been found.

Say or play the second set of words. This time, students should point at a complete group or to all the correct places.

Say or play the tape with the words in context. Students point to the correct part of the picture. In this case, there is only one correct place.

Tapescript

Presenter:	Theme 4 Culture and Civilization Lesson 1 **A Listen and point.**
Voices:	a man a woman a boy a girl a child an adult a female person a male person an old person a young person
Voices:	boys girls men women children adults females males friends
Voices:	One man is talking. The women are working. There are two boys. There are four girls. I can see eight adults in the pictures. There are two children in the picture. There are nine females in the pictures. I can see five males.

Exercise B

Demonstrate the activity to the students. They must find and circle different items in the pictures. Draw circles on the board, showing that circles can be inside other circles, or join up different parts of the pictures.

Say or play the sentences. Feed back, ideally onto an OHT of the page on which you can mark the correct circles.

Tapescript

Presenter: B Listen and find.
Voice: Circle one person.
Circle one boy.
Circle the girls.
Circle the boys.
Circle the women.
Circle the men.
Circle the adults.
Circle the children.
Circle the people.
Circle the male people.
Circle the female people.

Methodology note

This activity demonstrates that an item can belong to more than one group, a basic point in set theory and important in vocabulary learning. The physical act of drawing the circles may help a kinaesthetic learner to remember the relevant word.

Exercise C

Ask *How many boys are there in the picture?* Elicit the correct answer (2). Point out that students must count aloud in English. Test this with the next question: *How many women are there in the pictures?* (5) Ask students to answer the remaining questions chorally, then individually.

How many girls are there in the pictures? (4)
How many adults are there? (8)
How many children are there? (6)
How many people are there? (14)
How many male people are there? (5)
How many female people are there? (9)

Exercise D

Show students how one circle can contain two categories, e.g., *There are eight adults. There are five women and three men.*

Show students how one person can be in two categories.
She is a woman and she is female.

Say or play the sentences. Students say *True* or *False*. If it is false, ask for a correction, but do not insist on a full sentence, just correction of the numbers.

Answers

1 True
2 True
3 True
4 False: four female children

Tapescript

Presenter: D Listen. True or false?
Voice: 1 There are eight adults. There are five women and three men.
2 There are fourteen people. There are five male people and nine female people.
3 There are six children, four girls and two boys.
4 There aren't any female children.

Exercise E

Go round the class, repeating the various points and getting students to give themselves ticks for getting the people right, and praising for answering questions appropriately.

Closure

Help individual students who struggled during the lesson and allow them to leave when they can get most of the points correct immediately.

Lesson 2: Listening

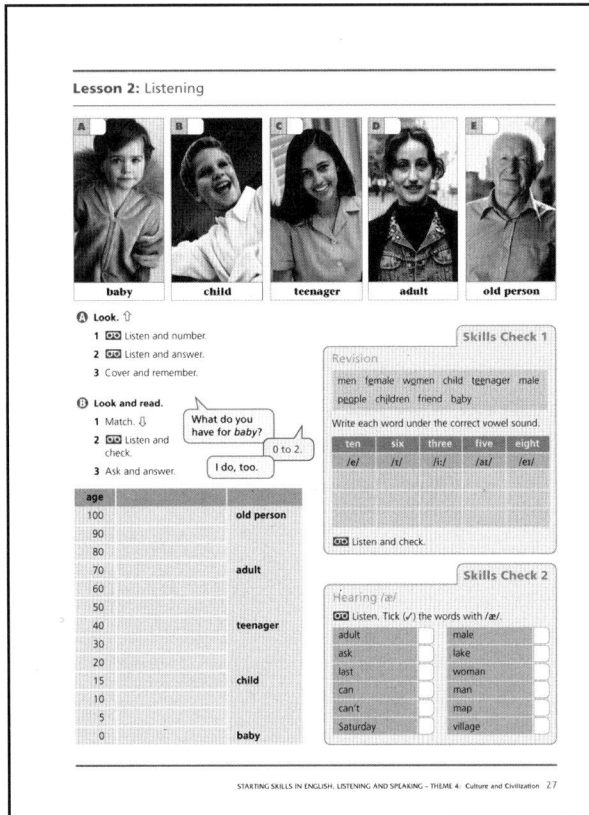

Introduction

Quickly revise the key words from the unit, especially the ones with irregular plurals, i.e., *man / men, woman / women, child / children*, e.g., say *man* and students should point to one of the men. Say *men* and they should point at the group. Also put the words in context, e.g., *Where are the men?* Revise *How many*. Remind students about counting in English.

Exercise A

1 Refer students to the five pictures. Set for individual work and pairwork checking. Play the tape. Students number the pictures. Feed back. Use language from the previous theme, e.g., *What's top left? Where's the old person?* etc.
2 Play the first question as an example. Elicit an answer chorally. Students should be able to make good sentences. Continue with the other questions.

Repeat, directing the question at individuals each time.
3 Ask students to cover their pictures and try to remember the location and details of each picture, e.g., *Top left there is a baby. She is 18 months old.*, etc.

Answers

1   A 3
    B 5
    C 1
    D 2
    E 4
2   1 She's 18 months old.
    2 He's 10 years old.
    3 She's 13.
    4 She's about 35.
    5 He's 80.

Tapescript

Presenter:	Lesson 2
	A 1 Listen and number.
Voice 1:	1 How old are you?
Girl:	Thirteen.
Voice 1:	Ah, so you're a teenager now.
Voice 2:	2 She is a nurse. She works in a hospital. She's about 35.
Voice 1:	3 What a lovely baby! How old is she?
Voice 2:	She's 18 months.
Man:	4 It's strange, you know. I'm 80, but I don't feel like an old person.
Woman 1:	5 Do you have any children?
Woman 2:	Yes, I have one child. He's 10.
Presenter:	**A 2 Listen and answer.**
Voice:	1 How old is the baby?
	2 How old is the boy?
	3 What about the teenager?

4 Is the woman about 50?
5 Is the old person about 60?

Exercise B

Refer students to the ages in the table. Revise numbers. Explain that they are going to hear a mini-lecture about the words in Exercise A. The lecture is about British culture. Explain the idea or get students to look up the word *culture* in a bilingual dictionary. When do we use the word *baby*? Elicit possible ages, e.g., *from 0 to 2*. Demonstrate how you can mark this on the set of numbers.

1 Put students in pairs to think and match. Make sure they use a pencil or just talk about it.
2 Play the tape. Do not feed back at this point.
3 Refer students to the speech bubbles. Put students into pairs to compare answers. Monitor, but do not confirm or correct. Feed back, building up the table on the board. Make sure students can say *zero* or *nought* for *0*. Point out the derivation of *teenager* by revising the numbers from *13* to *19*. Point out also that we can further subdivide ages by using the adjective *young* to form the phrases *young baby, young child, young adult*. We do not tend to use *young* with *teenager*, however. We only use *old* with *person*. We do not say, e.g., *an old child* (although we could say *older*, which is above the level of the students here). Finally, erase the table from the board and get students to close their books and make a new table in their notebooks, perhaps using colours for the different age groups.

Answers
baby: 0–2
child: 2–12
teenager: 13–19
adult: 20–100

Tapescript

Presenter: B 2 Listen and check.
Lecturer: In British culture, we use the word *baby* for the first 18 months to 2 years of life. Then the baby becomes a *child*. We use the word *child* for boys and girls between the ages of 2 and 12. Then we have a special word – *teenager*. The word comes from the numbers between 13 and 19. They all end in *teen*. So a person who is 13, 14, 15, and so on, is a *teen-ager*. Finally, we have the word *adult*. We use the word for people from 20 up to, well, 100. But sometimes we say *He is old* or *He is an old man* for someone over 65 or 70.

Methodology note

At one time, bilingual dictionaries were considered the curse of the ELT classroom, but gradually, people have realised that they do provide a short cut to students understanding key concepts. In this lesson, *culture* cannot easily be explained by mime or pictures. Translation quickly does the job. Beware of bilingual dictionaries, however, where there is a strong element of connotation that may not be carried by the equivalent word in the students' L1. For example, *teenager* probably does not translate very well (see Language and culture note). In Arabic, for example, *teenager* may be rendered as *murahiq*, but this is also the translation for *adolescent*, which surely has a very different sociocultural meaning in English.

Language and culture note

We talk about *teen culture* in English, perhaps because there is a convenient way of referring to the period from 13 to 19. In languages without such a clear set of consecutive ages, there is often no specific word for this period – *children* become *adults* without any named period in between – so be prepared for students to need the idea of the intermediate term to be explained. Even in British culture, 18- and 19-year-olds do not, in many cases, think of themselves as *teenagers,* but as *young adults.*

Closure

Refer students to Revision Skills Check 1. Check the pronunciation of the example words.
1   Elicit the words from the students and correct the pronunciation of the (stressed) vowel sound.
2   Give students time to try to place the words in the correct column.
3   Say or play the words for students to identify.

Feed back, building up the table on the board. Point out the unusual sound / sight relationships, i.e., *people, friend, female,* and the change of vowels in *woman – women* and *child – children.* Elicit some other words for each group.

Answers

ten	six	three	five	eight
/e/	/ɪ/	/iː/	/aɪ/	/eɪ/
men	*women*	*female*	*child*	*male*
friend	*children*	*teenager*	*baby*	
		people		

Tapescript

Presenter: Skills Check 1
             Listen and check.
Voice: men
             female
             women
             child
             teenager
             male
             people
             children
             friend
             baby

Refer students to Skills Check 2. Model the target sound. Play the tape.

Feed back, building up the table on the board. Point out that *can* is also pronounced *cn* sometimes. Ask students if they can see any patterns.

Answers

adult	✓	male	
ask		lake	
last		woman	
can	✓	man	✓
can't		map	✓
Saturday	✓	village	

Possible patterns:
a sometimes = target sound, but students must learn any words with *a* because there are many other possible sounds.

Tapescript

Presenter: Skills Check 2
             Listen. Tick the words with /æ/.
Voice: adult
             ask
             last
             can
             can't
             Saturday
             male
             lake
             woman
             man
             map
             village

Lesson 3: Speaking

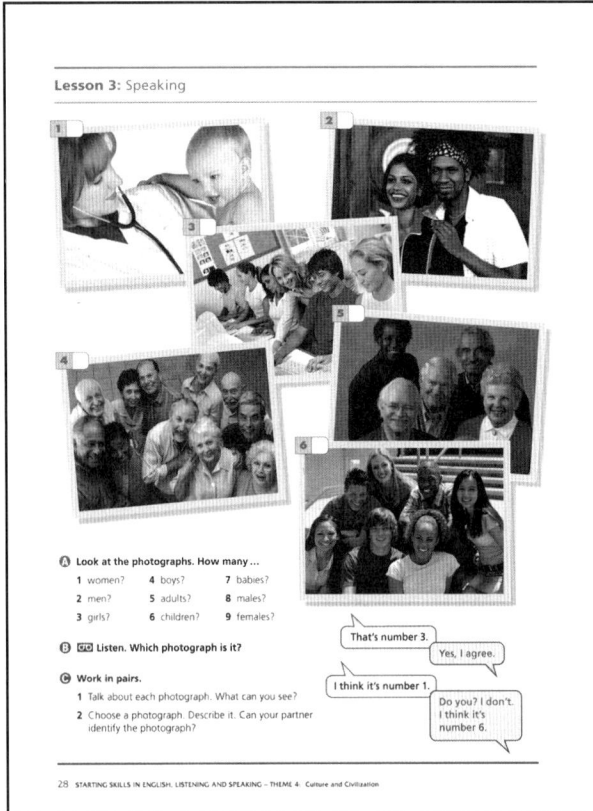

Exercise A

Refer students to the photographs. Set for pairwork. Elicit answers. Feed back, pointing out the correct number in each case.

Answers

1	10	4	5	7	1
2	10	5	20	8	15 (excluding baby)
3	7	6	5	9	17 (excluding baby)

Methodology note

Check that students are stressing the first syllable of the two-syllable words. Do not let them get away with full vowels on the unstressed syllables in the following words:

woman, women, children: unstressed vowel reduced to /ə/
babies: unstressed vowel reduced to /ɪ/

Make sure also that they are saying the clusters with reasonable accuracy as follows:

adults: /l/ and /t/ and /s/
children: /l/ and /d/ and /r/
girls: /l/ and /z/

Make sure they are also saying the blend /tʃ/ correctly.

Introduction

Draw a stick man on the board and say *a man*. Draw a second man and elicit *two men*. Say *a woman* and elicit *two women*. Continue with:

 an adult
 a child
 a boy
 a baby
 a teenager
 a girl
 a friend
 a person

Alternatively, if you have time, cut out and take in pictures of people in various combinations and flash them to elicit, e.g., *a man and two women*.

Work on the irregular plurals and the /s/ and /z/ plural sound.

Exercise B

Tell students they are going to hear descriptions of the photographs. They must identify the correct photograph in each case. Point out that they can feed back by saying where the correct photograph is as well as by saying its number, e.g., *top left, top middle*, etc.

Set each item for individual work and pairwork checking. Play the first text as an example. Elicit ideas, then confirm. Work through the ways that the students can talk about their ideas in the speech bubbles. Continue, pausing after each description for students to discuss their answers.

Methodology note

There is extraneous information that the students do not need to understand to be able to identify the pictures. This is the first direct work on tolerance of ambiguity, which is a basic element in good language learning. We will never understand everything that is said to us in a foreign language – we must try to cope with the information we do understand.

Answers
1. Picture 3 – top middle
2. Picture 2 – top right
3. Picture 6 – bottom right
4. Picture 1 – top left
5. Picture 4 – bottom left
6. Picture 5 – middle right

Tapescript
Presenter: Lesson 3
B Listen. Which photograph is it?

Voice:
1. There are five children in the picture. They are with a woman. I think she is their teacher.

2. There are two people in the picture. There's a man and a woman. They might be brother and sister, or maybe they are married.

3. There are seven people in the picture. They are teenagers. I think they're students. They are sitting outside a building. It's probably a college.

4. There are two people in the picture. There is a woman. She is holding a baby. She is a doctor. I don't think she's the baby's mother.

5. There are a lot of old people in the picture. They look very happy. Maybe they are old friends.

6. There are five people in the picture. There are three men and two women. They are all quite old. One of the men is wearing glasses.

Exercise C

At the bare minimum, students should be able to use the target language from this theme, but they should also be able to bring some other language to bear on the problem, such as clothes, colours and action verbs. Monitor and assist.

Methodology note

There is an approach to ELT called Community Language Learning (CLL). In this approach, students decide what they want to say, then ask the teacher to help them to say it. This approach accords with the principle that students learn when they want to say something or understand something. You might try a CLL approach to this activity, helping students to say what they want to say. CLL works particularly well if you speak the language of your students, but it can work through a combination of mime and trial and error.

Closure

Refer students to other pages of the course with pictures of people. Elicit who is in each picture using the target language.

Lesson 4: Speaking

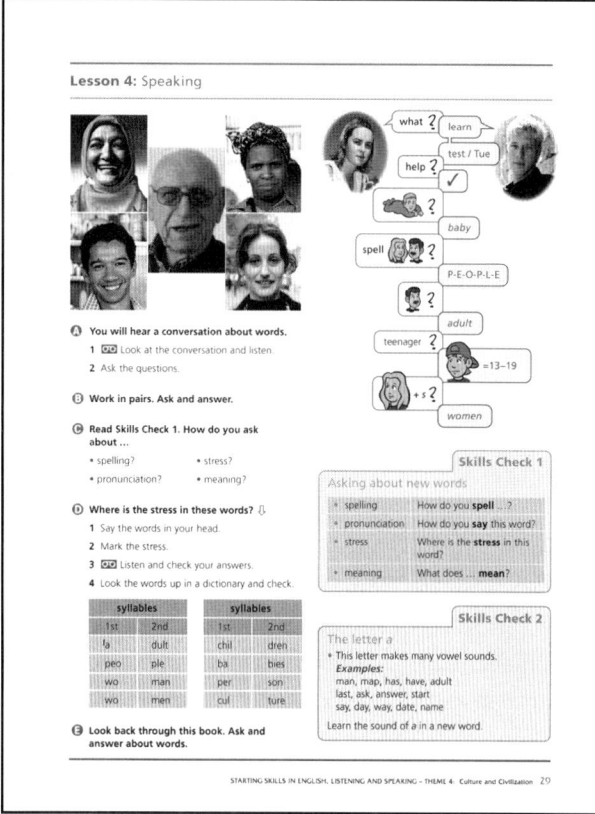

Exercise A

Refer students to the pictures near the dialogue. Elicit words, especially from this theme. Ask students for some ideas on what the people are saying, but do not confirm or correct.

1 Play the tape. Pause at each [PAUSE] for students to think about the previous exchange.
2 Go through the first exchange. Practise it with a student, then put the students into pairs to practise. Elicit all the other questions from the student, using the prompts, e.g., picture of baby = *What do you call this in English?* Monitor and assist. Feed back by eliciting, then playing the tape again, from *What do you call this in English?* Check / Correct pronunciation and intonation.

Tapescript

Presenter:	Lesson 4
	A 1 **Look at the conversation and listen.**
Female student:	What are you doing?
Male student:	I'm learning these words. We have a test on Tuesday.
Female student:	Can I help you?
Male student:	Yes, thanks.
	[PAUSE]
Female student:	What do you call this in English?
Male student:	It's a baby.
	[PAUSE]
Female student:	How do you spell *people*?
Male student:	P-E-O-P-L-E
Female student:	P-E-O-...?
Male student:	P-L-E
	[PAUSE]
Female student:	How do you say this word?
Male student:	'Adult.
Female student:	A'dult?
Male student:	No, 'adult. The stress is on the first syllable.
	[PAUSE]
Female student:	What does *teenager* mean?

Introduction

Take in pictures of groups of men, women, babies, etc., and ask students to say what they can see, e.g., *There are three men and two women.*
OR
Build up a drawing of stick people on the board with men, women, boys, girls and elderly people and, as you add each new drawing, ask students to describe the picture. Your final drawing could look something like this:

Male student:	It's a person from the age of 13 to 19.
	[PAUSE]
Female student:	What is the plural of *woman*?
Male student:	Women.
Female student:	How do you spell that?
Male student:	W-O-M-E-N
Female student:	And how do you say it?
Male student:	'Women.
Female student:	Well done.
Male student:	Thanks.
Female student:	Not at all.

Exercise B

Work through the answers to the questions. Put students in pairs to ask and answer. Feed back by getting different pairs to do each exchange.

Exercise C

Refer students to Skills Check 1. Feed back, eliciting the sentences from students chorally then individually.

Methodology note

Note that students have not seen the full sentences until this point. This is deliberate, to ensure that they are using their aural memory first, before getting bogged down in the sound / sight relationships or the grammar of the target structures.

Exercise D

Highlight the exchange about *adult*. Say the word with the stress in the wrong place, as on the tape the first time.

1. Set for individual work.
2. Demonstrate how to mark the stress with a vertical line. Point out that dictionaries often mark stress in this way.
3. Play the tape. Do not confirm or correct.
4. Set for individual work and pairwork checking. Feed back, building up the table on the board.

Answers

'peo	ple
'wo	man
'wo	men
'chil	dren
'ba	bies
'per	son
'cul	ture

Methodology note

Although the word *syllable* has been used before, students may not know what it means. Write the example word *adult* on the board and show how it can be split into two syllables. Point out that in two-syllable words in English, one syllable is stressed and the other is swallowed. Demonstrate rather than explain!

Tapescript

Presenter:	D 3 Listen and check your answers.
Voice:	adult
	people
	woman
	women
	children
	babies
	person
	culture

> **Language and culture note**
>
> Native speakers of English only hear stressed syllables. They identify the word from this syllable and the context. Thus, they only hear *mon* in the sentence *I went to the bank to get some money.* However, they know it is not *monkey, monks* or *Monday* from context.

Exercise E

Demonstrate how to do the activity. Ask about some words from previous themes. Put students into pairs. Explain that they should only ask about words where they have forgotten meaning, pronunciation or stress. Monitor and assist.

Closure

Work through Skills Check 2. Ask students to guess the pronunciation of these words then check in their dictionaries:

barn
bay
ban

THEME 5: They Made Our World

General note
By the end of this theme, students should be able to hear and identify, in isolation and in context, the following words linked with transport. They should also be able to say them with reasonable pronunciation and use them in simple S V O A sentences, e.g., *I want to ride my bicycle.*

bicycle	go
boat	plane
bus	road
car	sail
come	ship
drive	street
fly	train

Lesson 1: Listening

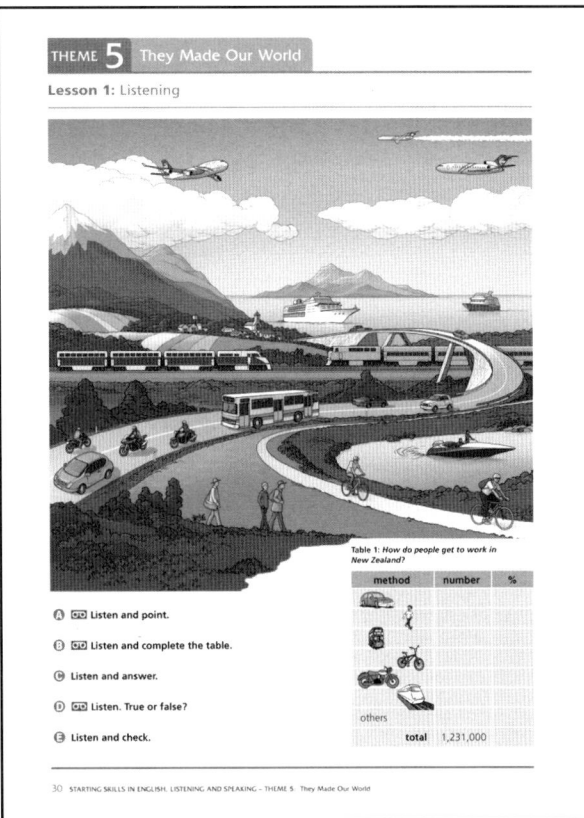

Introduction

Refer students to the picture. Focus on items in the picture from previous themes, including colours, e.g., *Find a lake, mountain, village. What's green in the picture? What colour are the clouds?* etc.

Ask *What can you see on the left / right / at the top / at the bottom / in the middle?* Elicit answers, but do not confirm or correct.

Exercise A

Say *OK. Let's check these words.* Say or play the tape with the words in isolation. Students point to the correct part of the picture.

Say or play the tape with the words in context. Students point to the correct part of the picture. In this case, there is only one correct place.

Tapescript
Presenter: Theme 5 They Made Our World
Lesson 1
A Listen and point.
Voices: a bicycle
a boat
a bus
a car
a plane
a ship
a train
a road
a lake
the sky
the sea
tracks

Voices: There is a boat on the lake.
There are four cars on the road.
I go to work by bus.
How many planes are there in the picture?
Where's the ship going?
Have you got a bicycle?
Are there many people on the train?
Do you like walking?

Exercise B

Refer students to the table. Read the question. If possible, show the location of New Zealand on a map. Say the method of transport and get students to tell you the place in the table, e.g.,
    You: *Car.*
    Students: *One* or *First.*

Repeat for three or four of the other methods, randomly, with the whole class responding, then continue asking individual students.

Refer students to the final entry: *others*. Ask students to suggest some other methods of transport.

Refer students to the first line of the table and play the first part of the tape. Elicit the number and show students how to write it in the space.

Play Part 2 of the tape, pausing where necessary for students to write the relevant number. Students compare in pairs.

Feed back, ideally onto an OHT of the table. Make sure students have used the comma correctly in the numbers.

Refer students to the last column of the table. Elicit the meaning of the symbol % – per cent or percentage – and demonstrate that it means *over 100*. You can do this by showing that the symbol has the *00* of hundreds and the line of division. Ask students what percentage of people go to work by car in New Zealand. Elicit ideas. Show them that the answer will be 1,000,000 divided by the total (1,231,000).

Play Part 3. Check that students have correctly identified the number. Check particularly that they have heard and can write the decimal number correctly. Continue with Part 4.

Answers

method	number	%
car	1,000,000	81.2
walking	93,000	7.6
bus	52,000	4.2
bicycle	41,000	3.3
motorbike	17,000	1.4
train	15,000	1.2
others	13,000	1.1
total	1,231,000	100.0

Tapescript

Presenter: B Listen and complete the table. Part 1

Voice: How do most people get to work? According to a recent survey, most people in New Zealand go to work by car. The researchers say that one million people go to work by car each day.

Presenter: Part 2

Voice: Walking is in second place. 93,000 people walk to work. In third place is the bus. 52,000 people go to work by bus each day. Nearly 60,000 people ride to work. 41,000 go by bicycle and 17,000 go by motorbike. Only 15,000 go by train. 13,000 people go to work by another method. For example, on rollerskates or on a skateboard!

Presenter: Part 3

Voice: We can look at these numbers in a different way. What percentage of people go to work by car in New Zealand? The answer is 81.2%. Here are the percentages for the other methods. Walking – 7.6%. Going by bus – 4.2%. Bicycle – 3.3%. Motorbike – 1.4%, and going by train – 1.2%. All the other methods added up to 1.1%.

Exercise C

Ask *How many people go to work by car in New Zealand?* Elicit the answer. (*1 million*)

Ask *What percentage of people go to work by car?* Elicit 81.2%. Make sure that students are saying the decimal point correctly.

Ask more questions about the information in the table in the same way. Elicit answers chorally then individually.

Exercise D

Put students into pairs. Make the following statement, then ask if it is true or false. Do not allow students to answer. Get them to tell their partner.
   The car is the most popular method. (True)
Feed back. If necessary, explain *popular*, i.e., many people like it. Get students to explain their answer: *It's in first place*.

Say or play the tape with the other questions, pausing after each one for students to discuss in pairs. Do not let students shout out the answers. Point out they must explain their answers as in the example.

Answers
The car is the most popular method.
True. It is in first place.

Walking is more popular than riding a bicycle.
True. It is in second place, riding a bicycle is in fourth place.

The bicycle is in third place.
False. It is in fourth place.

The train is not as popular as the bus.
True. It is in sixth place, and the bus is in third place.

Nearly 60,000 people ride to work.
True. Bicycle and motorbike.

Nearly 10% of people go by bicycle or motorbike.
False. Nearly 5% do that.

Tapescript

Presenter:		D Listen. True or false?
Voice:		The car is the most popular method.
		Walking is more popular than riding a bicycle.
		The bicycle is in third place.
		The train is not as popular as the bus.
		Nearly 60,000 people ride to work.
		Nearly 10% of people go by bicycle or motorbike.

Exercise E

Go round the class, repeating the various points and getting students to give themselves ticks for getting the methods right and for answering questions about the table appropriately.

Closure

Help individual students who struggled during the lesson and allow them to leave when they can get most of the points correct immediately.

Exercise B

Refer students to Table 2. Ask *Which is the fastest of these?* Mime, if necessary. Elicit ideas. Ask *How fast can a plane go?* Check or teach *speed*. Elicit some ideas and, eventually, add *kilometres per hour*. Make sure students understand the concept and the abbreviation *kph*. Go through the other methods, eliciting ideas. Do not confirm or correct.

Refer students to the blue box below the table on the left with the numbers. Explain that they are going to hear these numbers. Get some good students to say the numbers out loud. Make sure they are saying the numbers after the decimal point as separate items, e.g., *point eight three*, not *point eighty three*.

Refer students to the green box on the right with the dates. Explain that they are going to hear these dates. Get some of the good students to say the dates out loud.

Point out that the numbers are speeds. Put students into pairs to try to work out which goes with each method of transport in the table.

Play the tape. Students should mark up the lists of numbers and dates as they listen, then copy them into the correct place in the table.

Note that there are two numbers and two dates which are not used.

Answers

	speed (in kph)	date
plane	7,692.66	28/03/04
car	1,227.98	15/10/97
motorbike	518.45	14/07/90
train	515.30	18/05/90
bicycle	268.83	3/10/95

Tapescript

Presenter: B 2 Listen and check.

Voices: The record speed for a plane is 7,692.66 kilometres per hour. The record was set on 28th March, 2004.

The record speed for a car is 1,227.98 kilometres per hour. The record was set on 15th October, 1997.

The fastest speed for a motorbike is 518.45 kph. This record was set on 14th July, 1990.

On 18th May, 1990, a train travelled at 515.30 kph.

What is the record speed for a bicycle? 50 kph? 100? 200? On 3rd October, 1995, a bicycle travelled at 268.83 kilometres per hour. The bicycle was behind a car.

Methodology notes

1. Students have, until now, only formally revised the ordinals up to 9. They should, however, be able to remember or work out how to say the other ordinals in the dates.
2. Students have not formally revised how to write dates as DD MM YY. Point out that the second number is the number of the month, e.g., *05 = 5th month* or *May*. You may well have to revise this.

Closure

Refer students to Revision Skills Check 2. Check the pronunciation of the example words.

1. Elicit the words from the students and correct the pronunciation of the (stressed) vowel sound.
2. Give students time to try to place the words in the correct column.
3. Say or play the words for students to identify. Feed back, building up the table on the board. Point out that:
   - some words with /eɪ/ end in *a* + C + *e* and some have *ai* in the middle.
   - some words with /aɪ/ end in *i* + C + *e* and some end in *y*.

   Elicit some other words for each group.

Answers

six	tree	five	map	date
/ɪ/	/iː/	/aɪ/	/æ/	/eɪ/
ship	street	bi*c*ycle	track	plane
		drive		sail
		fly		train
		motor bike		

Tapescript

Presenter: Skills Check 2
Listen and check.
Voice: bicycle
drive
fly
plane
sail
ship
street
train
track
motorbike

Refer students to Skills Check 3. Model the target sound. Play the tape.

Feed back, building up the table on the board. Ask students if they can see any patterns.

Possible patterns:
The target sound can be made with *oa*, and *o* + C + *e*. Unfortunately, it can also be made with *o*.

Answers
With the target sound:
boat
don't
go
goes
motor
home
know
no
road
phone

With another sound:
do
does
how
now
long

Tapescript

Presenter: Skills Check 3
Listen. Tick the words with /əʊ/.
Voice: boat
do
does
don't
go
goes
motor
home
how
know
no
now
road
phone
long

Lesson 3: Speaking

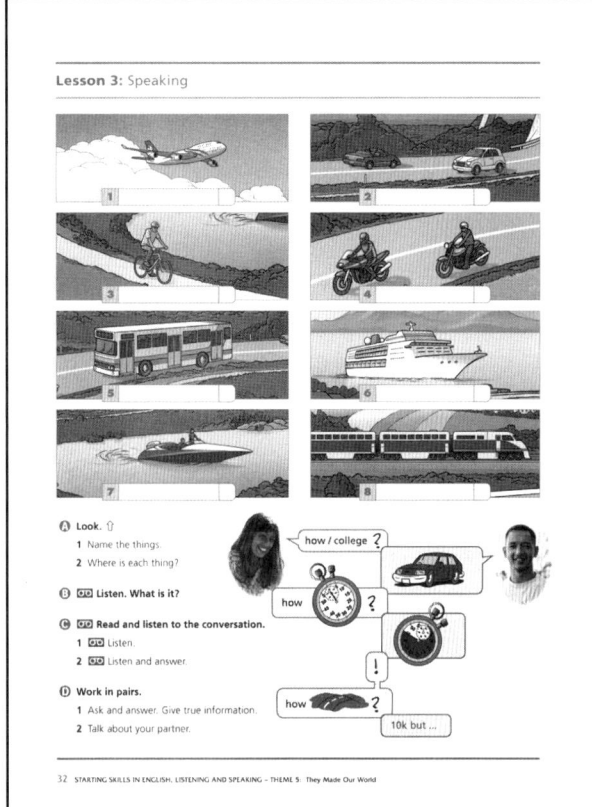

Introduction

Ask students: *How do you come to college / university / school every day?*

Elicit information. Build up a tally table on the board. Obviously, campus-based students will just say *walk*, but that's fine. In this case, you might like to teach the alternative *on foot*.

Ask students: *How long does it take?* Mime to indicate what this means, perhaps pointing at your watch and miming the minute hand going round.

Elicit information. Build up a tally table as before. In this case, give time slots, e.g.,
 <5 minutes
 6–10 minutes
 11–15, etc.

Ask students: *How far is it?* Mime as before, perhaps gradually widening your arms.

Exercise A

Refer students to the illustrations.

1 Elicit what each item is. Correct pronunciation as you go. Make sure students are not sounding the /r/ at the end of *car*, unless you sound it in your variety of English.
2 Ask about location of the items in two ways. Firstly, check that students can still use the location phrases: *at the top, on the left,* etc. Secondly, model the answer *The plane is in the sky.* Ask about the location of the other items and elicit similar sentences.

Answers
1 plane
2 car(s)
3 bicycle
4 motorbike(s)
5 bus
6 ship
7 boat
8 train

Methodology note

Use consistent mime to remind students of key vocabulary. For example, for *how long?* you can show the minute hand going round, for *how far?* you can gradually spread your arms. You might like to get students to copy the mime for a while whenever they use one of these expressions to help to fix it with an action. This may help kinaesthetic learners.

Exercise B

Tell students they are going to hear sounds. They must identify the correct item in each case. Set each item for pairwork checking. Play the first sound as an example. Elicit ideas, then confirm.

If you think your students would play along, say the names of the items and get them to make suitable sound effects.

> **Methodology note**
>
> This is mainly a bit of fun, but there is a serious language learning point. We can instantly 'name' sounds in our L1 because we associate the sound, not just with the item but with its name in English. This sort of activity attempts to create the same mental relationship between sounds and names in the L2.

Answers
1 motorbike
2 bus
3 car
4 plane
5 ship
6 train
7 boat
8 bicycle

Tapescript
Presenter: Lesson 3
B Listen. What is it?
Sound effects: 1 motorbike
2 bus
3 car
4 plane
5 ship
6 train
7 boat
8 bicycle

Exercise C

Ask students to look at the rebus conversation and try to work out what the people are saying. This should not be too difficult as you used the three questions in the introduction. Elicit ideas, but do not confirm or correct.

1 Play the conversation.
2 Play it again, pausing after each question for the students to answer, then play each reply for students to check.

Build up the questions on the board. Show that they all begin with *How*, but continue in different ways.

		do	you	get	to college	?
How	long	does	it	take	?	
	far	is	it	?		

Drill the questions. Make sure students are using falling intonation.

Get students to ask you the questions and give true answers. Get them to turn the information into an extended turn about you, i.e.,

He / She gets to college by car. It takes 30 minutes. It's about 20 kilometres.

Tapescript
Presenter: C 1 Listen.
Female student: How do you get to college?
Male student: I come by car.
Female student: How long does it take?
Male student: About 45 minutes.
Female student: 45 minutes! How far is it?
Male student: It's only about 10 kilometres. But the traffic is very bad.

Presenter: C 2 Listen and answer.
[REPEAT OF EXERCISE C1]

Exercise D

1. Set for pairwork. Monitor and assist. Make sure students are using falling intonation for these *Wh-* questions.
2. Remind students about the mini-text they made about you. Get students to construct mini-texts about their partner.

Closure

1. Elicit mini-texts from one of each pair.
2. Get students to do sound effects for other students to guess.

Lesson 4: Speaking

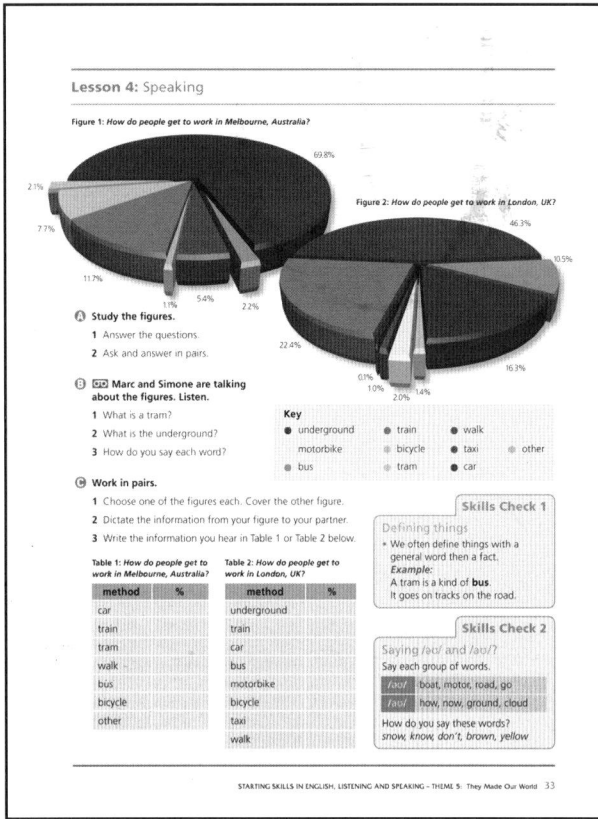

Introduction

Take in pictures of the different methods of transport, ideally from different countries. Include some famous ones like London buses, the bullet train of Japan, a Harley Davidson motorbike and different types of car. Flash the pictures and get instant responses. If there are different combinations of vehicles, so much the better.

Finish, if possible, with the yellow cabs of New York. This will lead you into *taxi*. If you have no picture, just say *... and of course, the taxi*. Ask *What's a taxi?* and elicit possible definitions. Then say *It's a kind of car. People pay to ride in it*. Mime to make the meaning clear. This previews the later definition activity.

Exercise A

Refer students to the two figures. Teach the word *figure*. Say that we use it for pictures, graphs, etc., in a text.

1. Ask quick checking questions, e.g.,
    *   *Which figure is about people in Australia?*
    *   *What is the other figure about?*
    *   *What percentage of people go to work by car in London?*
    *   *What about in Melbourne?*
    *   *What does the purple part of Figure 1 show?*
    *   *What about the green part of Figure 2?* etc.
    For the moment, avoid dealing with the new words *tram* and *underground*.
2. Put students in pairs to ask and answer similar questions. Monitor and assist.

Exercise B

Set for individual work and pairwork checking. Play the tape. Give plenty of time for students to discuss. Feed back.

Ask students:
> *Do you have trams in your country? Where?*
> *Do you have underground trains? Where?*

Refer students to Skills Check 1 and highlight the structure of the definition.

      general word   fact about the items
*A tram is a kind of **bus**. It goes on tracks on the road.*

Elicit the definition of *the underground* in the same way.

Ask about the other words. Try to elicit definitions like:
> *A van is a kind of car. You can carry things in it.*

Tapescript

Presenter:	Lesson 4
	B Marc and Simone are talking about the figures. Listen.
Marc:	Simone?
Simone:	Yes?
Marc:	How do you say this word?
Simone:	Which word?
Marc:	This one. T-R-A-M.
Simone:	*Tram.*

Marc: *Tram*. Right. What does it mean?
Simone: A tram is a kind of bus. It goes on tracks on the road.
Marc: Oh, yes. I know. What about this one – *under'ground*.
Simone: Oh, yes. The *'underground*.
Marc: Where is the stress?
Simone: It's on the first syllable.
Marc: *'Underground*.
Simone: That's right.
Marc: So what does it mean?
Simone: It's a kind of train. It goes under the ground.
Marc: Oh, right. Like the subway in New York.
Simone: Yes, and the métro in Paris.

Methodology note

Circumlocution is a key speaking skill. If you can tell your interlocutor that the item you are thinking of is a kind of something else, they will immediately have the correct frame of reference and are much more likely to be able to understand and help you to the exact word. It is, therefore, extremely valuable to teach beginners / false beginners apparently low-cover words, hypernyms like *furniture / food / clothing / transport / sport*, because they can use these when they don't know the precise term.

Exercise C

Follow the instructions as written. Make sure students are making full sentences, e.g.,
> *69.8 per cent of people go to work by car.*
> *The percentage for the train is 11.7%.*
> *The tram is in third place with 7.7%.*
> etc.

Monitor and assist students in pronouncing the numbers, especially the decimal point.

Feed back by building up the table from each figure.

Answers

Table 1: *How do people get to work in Melbourne, Australia?*

method	%
car	69.8
train	11.7
tram	7.7
walk	5.4
bus	2.2
bicycle	2.1
other	1.1

Table 2: *How do people get to work in London, UK?*

method	%
underground	46.3
train	22.4
car	16.3
bus	10.5
motorbike	2.0
bicycle	1.4
taxi	1.0
walk	0.1

Language and culture note

If a series of numbers has a decimal point, we often say, e.g., *two point zero* rather than just *two*.

Closure

1 Ask students what *other* could mean in Table 1. (Answer: *motorbike*, *skateboard*, etc., even *plane* perhaps!)
2 Work through the sounds in Skills Check 2. Ask students to guess the pronunciation of these words, then check in their dictionaries.
> *show* (/əʊ/)
> *clown* (/aʊ/)
> *tow* (/əʊ/)
> *bow* (They should find that both are possible, with different meanings.)

THEME 6 Art and Literature

General note
By the end of this theme, students should be able to hear and identify, in isolation and in context, the following words linked with art and literature. They should also be able to say them with reasonable pronunciation and use them in simple S V O sentences where O = object pronoun, e.g., *She wrote it in 1950.*

Art
architecture – architect
painting – painter
sculpture – sculptor

Literature
biography – biographer
novel – novelist
play – playwright
poem – poet

Lesson 1: Listening

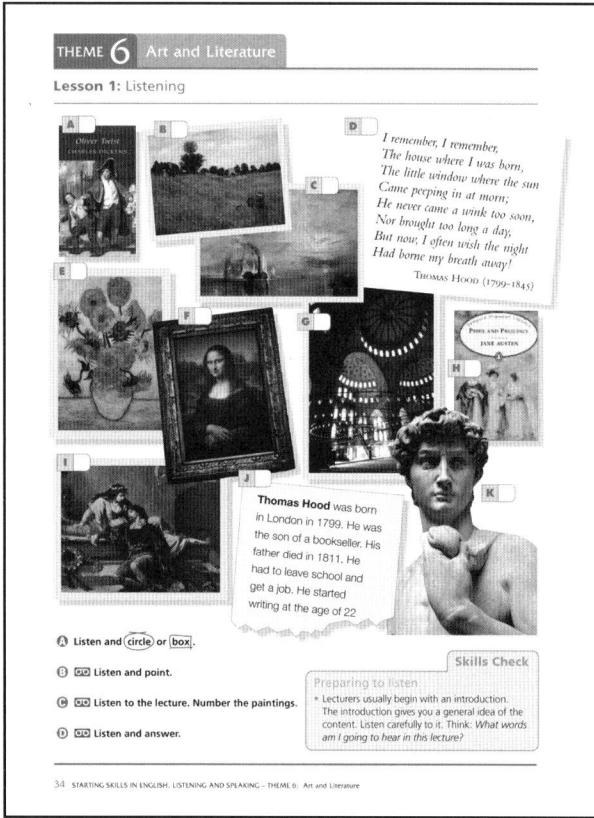

Introduction

Find on the Internet, and take in, images of the following.
- Leonardo da Vinci's *Mona Lisa*
- Michelangelo's *David* (just the head and shoulders)
- Monet's *Corn Poppies*
- Van Gogh's *Sunflowers*
- Turner's *The Fighting Temeraire*
- The Blue Mosque in Turkey
- The Pyramids

It would also be good to have a copy of a novel, a poem, a play and a biography.

Say *We're going to talk about these things today*. Pin or stick the images on the board and arrange the books on your desk. If students want to name the items, the artists, etc., encourage this, but do not put students on the spot.

Point to each example of art and say *Art*. Hold up each example of literature and say *Literature*. Do not ask students to repeat the words, but allow them to do so if they wish.

Methodology note

On the face of it, words like *art* and *literature* are not high-cover words and would certainly not feature in a list of the first 500 words in English. However, they are extremely useful in circumlocution, e.g., *It's a kind of art*, and, as noted before, hypernyms such as these can be more valuable to the language learner than the names for specific items, e.g., *painting* or *novel*.

Exercise A

Refer students to the pictures. Focus on items in the pictures from previous themes, including colours.

Say *Circle the art*. Allow students time to circle the items.

Say *Box the literature*. Allow time as before.

Answers
They can include all the art items in one circle and all the literature items in one box, or circle and box each item separately.

Exercise B

Hold up individual items from your realia or point at them. Name them. As before, if students name the items correctly before you do, acknowledge that, but do not insist that students repeat each item. Refer students to the pictures on the page.

Say or play the tape with the words in isolation. Students point to the part of the picture.

Say or play the tape with the words in context. Students point to the correct part of the picture.

Tapescript

Presenter: Theme 6 Art and Literature
Lesson 1
B Listen and point.

Voices: painting
sculpture
architecture
novel
play
poem
biography

Voices: Do you like the plays of William Shakespeare?
Have you read the new biography of Charles Dickens?
I love this poem. It's by Thomas Hood.
I'm very interested in architecture.
This sculpture is very famous.
What a lovely painting? Who is the painter?
Who wrote this novel?

Exercise C

Ask students: *How many paintings are there?* Elicit that there are four. Refer students to the Skills Check.

Set for individual work and pairwork checking. Play Part 1 of the tape – the introduction. Monitor and assist, modeling pronunciation of predicted words but not insisting on students producing the words correctly. Feed back, modeling the words for the whole class, but, as before, do not fall into a *listen and repeat* activity as the point here is preparing the students aurally for the words they might hear, rather than correcting and improving their own pronunciation.

Set for individual work and pairwork checking. Play the rest of the lecture.

Feed back, playing the part of a confused student as follows.
What did she call the first kind of painting?
Which painting is that?
How do you spell that? (Clearly, they don't know how. They will have to guess.)
What examples did she give?

Answers

Elicit any useful words from the pictures.

F 1 portrait

B 2 landscape

C 3 seascape

E 4 still life

Methodology notes

1. As mentioned before, it is clear that listening helps speaking, but not so clear that speaking helps listening. It may even be that a focus on speaking in a predominantly listening lesson muddies the aural waters.
2. This is an exercise in tolerance of ambiguity. It is not possible to teach students everything that they are going to hear in a lecture room, so they will always be coping with lack of understanding to a greater or lesser degree. They must not panic when this happens, but they need to be trained to deal with the situation calmly, to understand what they can understand and to fill in the blanks later – see the Skills Check in the next lesson.

Tapescript

Presenter: C Listen to the lecture. Number the paintings.
Part 1

Female lecturer: There are three main kinds of art in Western culture. There is painting, sculpture and architecture. However, I'm not going to talk about sculpture or architecture today. I'm going to concentrate on painting.

Presenter: Part 2

Female lecturer: There are four main kinds of painting in Western culture. Firstly, there are portraits. A portrait is a painting of a person. You can usually see just the head and shoulders, but sometimes you can see the whole person. The person is usually looking out of the painting at you. Many portraits show famous people, but the most famous portrait of all shows the face of an unknown woman. It is called the *Mona Lisa*. It is by the Italian painter, Leonardo da Vinci.

The second kind of painting is the landscape. A landscape shows a piece of land – perhaps it is a mountain, or a river, or trees or a field of flowers. Sometimes there are people in a landscape painting, but they are not important. The painter is interested in the land itself. Claude Monet, the French painter, did many landscapes, including *Corn Poppies*.

The third kind of painting is the seascape. A seascape painting is similar to a landscape, but, of course, the important thing is the sea. Sometimes there are boats or ships in the picture, but sometimes we can just see the sea, calm or stormy. The English painter, Turner, did a lot of seascapes, including *The Fighting Temeraire*.

The fourth kind of painting is called a still life. In a still life painting, we can see some flowers or some fruit – apples, oranges, pears, grapes. There are some very famous still life paintings, including *Sunflowers* by the Dutch painter, Vincent Van Gogh.

Exercise D

Put students into pairs. Ask the first question: *How many main kinds of paintings are there in Western culture?* Do not allow students to answer. Get them to tell their partner. Feed back. The correct answer is *four*.

Say or play the tape with the other questions, pausing after each one for students to discuss in pairs. Do not let students shout out the answers. Point out that they must tell each other.

Feed back. Don't worry if they cannot pronounce the words properly. They probably only have aural memory to work on as most of the answers are likely to be new words.

Answers
1 four
2 Any one of the four kinds is acceptable.
3 a portrait
4 a landscape
5 fruit, flowers, or specific examples
6 a seascape

Tapescript
Presenter: D Listen and answer.
Voice: 1 How many main kinds of paintings are there in Western culture?
2 Can you name one of the kinds?
3 What kind of painting is Picture 1?
4 What about Picture 2?
5 What can you see in a still life painting?
6 What kind of painting has boats or ships?

Closure

Ask students which kind of art they like best. Repeat with kinds of painting, then with kinds of literature. You can try asking them why, but it is unlikely that they have the language to explain. However, if you speak the students' language well, you can use a Community Language Learning approach, i.e., get them to tell you in their own language, then paraphrase it in simple English and teach them the way to express the idea.

Lesson 2: Listening

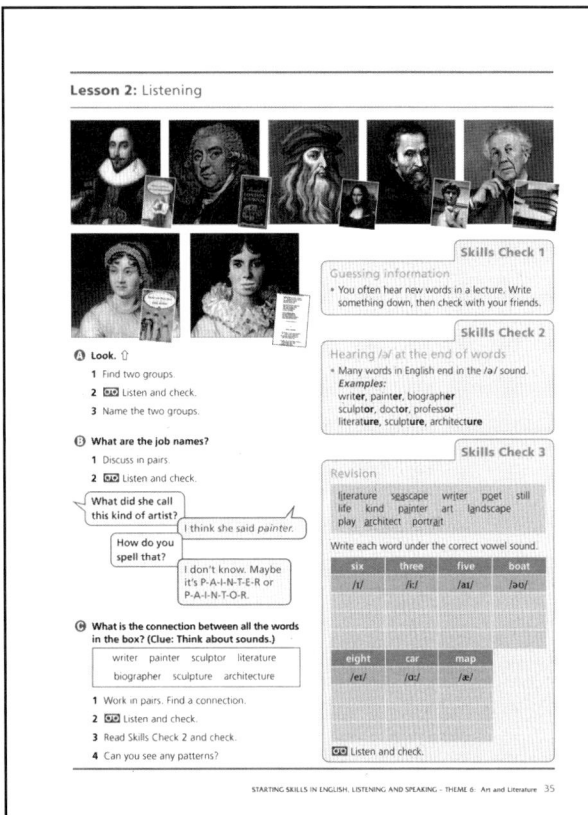

Answers

A 1 novel
J 2 biography
I 3 play
D 4 poem

Tapescript

Presenter: Lesson 2
Introduction

Female lecturer: Every culture has its own art and literature. I'm not going to talk about art today. I'm going to talk about literature in Western culture.

Presenter: The lecture

Female lecturer: There are four main kinds of literature. Firstly, there are novels. A novel is a story. Novels often tell the story of a person's life, but the story is not true. The most famous novelist in English literature is Charles Dickens. One of his most famous novels is *Oliver Twist*.
The second kind of literature is the biography. A biography is also the story of a person's life, but it is the life of a real person. There are biographies of every famous person in the world.
Thirdly, there are plays. A play is also a story. Actors bring the story to life in a theatre. The most famous playwright in English literature is William Shakespeare. He wrote many plays, including *Romeo and Juliet*.
Finally, there are poems. A poem is often about one idea. Many poems have words with similar sounds. We call this *rhyme*. For example, *say* and *play*, or *right* and *night*.

Introduction

Use the realia as before. On this occasion, say each word and get students to point or come up individually and touch or pick up the item. Explain that students are now going to hear a short lecture. Refer them to the Skills Check in Lesson 1 again.

Play the introduction. Ask students what they are going to hear about. Get them to identify the relevant pictures from Lesson 1. Ask them to think of possible words in pairs. Monitor and assist, modeling words that could be in the lecture.

Tell them to listen to the lecture and number the items as they are mentioned.

Set for individual work and pairwork checking. Play the rest of the lecture.

Exercise A

1 Refer students to the seven pictures. Ask them to make two groups and explain their grouping. Set for pairwork. Feed back on possible ideas, but do not confirm or correct.
2 Play the tape. Set for individual work and pairwork checking.
3 Feed back. Ask students for the names of the two groups.

Answers
The two groups are *artists* and *writers*.

Methodology note

Students have previously learnt, in Theme 1, about some job suffixes. Remind them of this and, in the feed back, point out that the names of the jobs are usually derived from a related word; in this case *art – artist; write – writer*. However, they previously learnt that 'verb' + 'suffix' = 'job', whereas here in the first case the root word is clearly a noun. This is just one example of how unproductive this kind of rule is in English for speakers / writers. It can only 'suggest' a possible way to build a word, not tell us exactly how to do it. This point is extended in Exercise B. However, as a listener / reader it can be more helpful. Suffixes such as *-ist* and *-or* are indicators that a word might be a job; thus, *flautist* and *author* might be understandable in context given this added information. Of course, there are words ending in *-ist* and *-or* which are not jobs, e.g., *communist, donor*, so, as with most patterns in English, it must be used with care.

Tapescript

Presenter: A 2 Listen and check.
Female lecturer: There are special names for people who make art or literature. For example, *painter, sculptor, poet*. But we can divide people into two groups. Firstly, there are the artists. This group contains painters, like Leonardo da Vinci, and sculptors, like Michelangelo. It also contains architects, like the American, Frank Lloyd Wright. Secondly, we have the writers. This group comprises novelists like the English woman, Jane Austen, and poets, like the American woman, Emily Dickinson. It also contains playwrights. The most famous playwright in the world is, of course, William Shakespeare. Finally, this group includes biographers. A biographer writes the story of another person's life, like James Boswell who wrote the story of Dr Johnson's life.

Exercise B

Remind students that they heard the special job names for the different artists and writers in the pictures. Elicit one or two. Use language from the speech bubbles and encourage students to do the same.

1 Put students in pairs to discuss the rest.
2 Play the tape again for students to check. Feed back, getting some possible ideas on the board. Confirm the correct spelling after some time. Point out the very unusual spelling of *wright* but, as this is a listening and speaking lesson, do not force students to learn the spelling at this point.

Answers
In order, from left to right:
Top: playwright, biographer, painter, sculptor, architect
Bottom: novelist, poet

Methodology note

Throughout this course, students are normally only allowed to listen to a tape once. This is a fundamental methodological point. In real life, we are rarely able to listen a second time, and offering this facility to students removes from them the need to develop coping strategies for one-time listening. However, in this case, they are listening for something different the second time, and therefore, arguably, it is allowable.

Tapescript

Presenter: B 2 Listen and check.
[REPEAT OF EXERCISE A2]

Exercise C

Refer students to the box of words. Set the whole activity for pairwork. Feed back, building up the group of words from Skills Check 2 in the three groups.

Answers

The patterns are:
- -er
- -or
- -ure

Point out that -er and -or are endings for names of jobs, although, as noted earlier, they do not only end job names.

Point out the /tʃ/ sound before the schwa with the final group.

Tapescript

Presenter: C 2 Listen and check.
Voice: writer
painter
sculptor
literature
biographer
sculpture
architecture

Closure

Refer students to Revision Skills Check 3. Check the pronunciation of the example words.

1. Elicit the words from the students and correct the pronunciation of the (underlined) vowel sound. Note that, on this occasion, the underlined vowel is not the stressed vowel.
2. Give students time to try to place the words in the correct column.
3. Say or play the words for students to identify.

Feed back, building up the table on the board. Elicit some other words for each group.

Answers

six	three	five	boat
/ɪ/	/iː/	/ai/	/əʊ/
l<u>i</u>terature	s<u>ea</u>scape	wr<u>i</u>ter	p<u>o</u>et
st<u>i</u>ll		l<u>i</u>fe	
		k<u>i</u>nd	

eight	car	map
/ei/	/ɑː/	/æ/
p<u>ai</u>nter	<u>a</u>rt	l<u>a</u>ndscape
pl<u>ay</u>	<u>a</u>rchitect	
portr<u>ai</u>t		

Tapescript

Presenter: Skills Check 3
Listen and check.
Voice: literature
seascape
writer
poet
still
life
kind
painter
art
landscape
play
architect
portrait

Lesson 3: Speaking

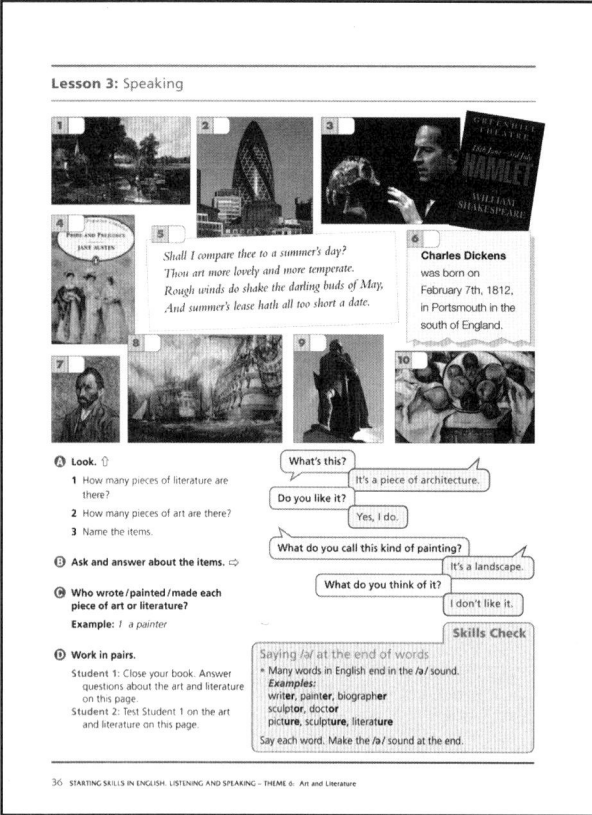

Introduction

Use the realia from the first two lessons. On this occasion, hold up or point to each item and get students to say the words, correcting pronunciation as you go.

Exercise A

Refer students to the pictures.

1 Ask the whole class, then get individual students to give the number of the pieces.
2 Repeat the procedure.
3 Elicit the names, chorally then individually. Students should give the specific name for each type of painting, e.g., *landscape*.

Answers
1 There are 4 pieces: 3, 4, 5, 6.
2 There are 6 pieces: 1, 2, 7–10.
3 The pieces are as follows:
   1 painting (landscape)
   2 architecture
   3 play
   4 novel
   5 poem
   6 biography
   7 painting (portrait)
   8 painting (seascape)
   9 sculpture
   10 painting (still life)

Exercise B

Refer students to the two four-line dialogues. Drill the exchanges using different interactional patterns, e.g., T–Ss, T–S1, half classes, S1–S2. Check the pronunciation of individual sounds and the intonation patterns of the questions.

Practise the dialogues with different items, i.e., hold up the book and point to different items and ask an individual student:
   What's this? then continue with the rest of the dialogue
OR
   What do you call this kind of art / literature / painting? then continue with the rest of the dialogue.
Put students in pairs to ask and answer in the same way.

Exercise C

Refer students to the Skills Check. Make sure students can say /ə/ chorally and individually at the end of the example words. Ask students for more words ending in /ə/. So far in this course, the following have been specifically taught, but of course you could suggest others: *answer, centre, computer, teenager, lecture*.

Work through the exercise example. Set for pairwork. Feed back orally.

Answers
1 a painter
2 an architect
3 a playwright
4 a novelist
5 a poet
6 a biographer
7 a painter
8 a painter
9 a sculptor
10 a painter

Exercise D

Refer students to the art and literature again. Ask a range of questions. Students use available linguistic resources to try to describe the items, e.g.,
> *What's the sculpture? It's a man,* etc.
> *What's the poem about? Love / May,* etc.
> *What's the piece of architecture?*
> *Is there a ship in the seascape?*
> *What kind of fruit is in the still life?*
> *What's the name of the play?* etc.

Put students into pairs to test each other.

Closure

Ask some high-speed questions about the pieces of art and literature, e.g., *Can you see something green? Which piece of art has a pear?* etc.

Lesson 4: Speaking

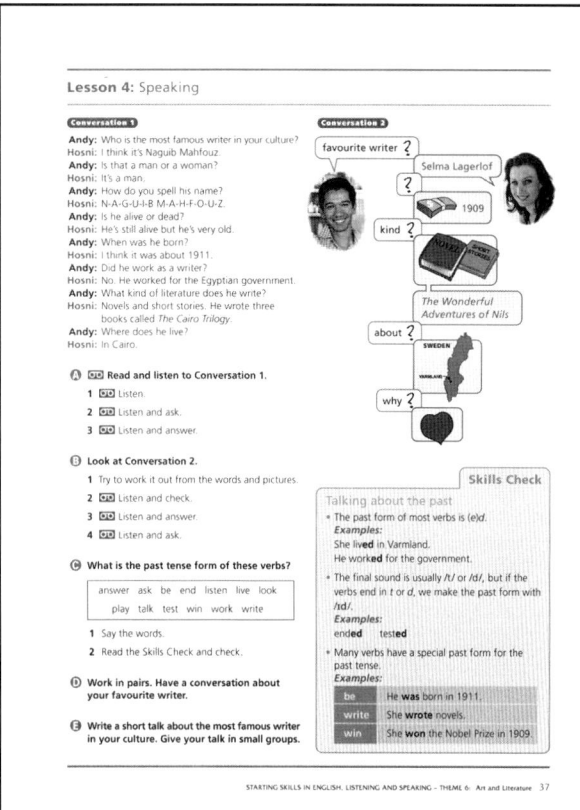

Introduction

Refer students to the art and literature in Lesson 3 again. Name individual items and get students to identify where the items appear, e.g., *ship – in the landscape painting*.

Exercise A

Refer students to Conversation 1.

1 Play the tape. Ask students to listen particularly to the questions.
2 Ask students to cover the conversation. Say *Who?* and prompt the first question. Play the question and the answer. Elicit the next question. If necessary, give a prompt. Repeat for each question.
3 Play the tape once more. Stop after each question and elicit the answer.

Put students into pairs to ask and answer the questions in Conversation 1. Monitor and assist. Correct pronunciation and intonation as appropriate.

Tapescript

Presenter:	Lesson 4	
	A 1 Listen.	
Andy:	Who is the most famous writer in your culture?	
Hosni:	I think it's Naguib Mahfouz.	
Andy:	Is that a man or a woman?	
Hosni:	It's a man.	
Andy:	How do you spell his name?	
Hosni:	N-A-G-U-I-B M-A-H-F-O-U-Z	
Andy:	Is he alive or dead?	
Hosni:	He's still alive, but he's very old.	
Andy:	When was he born?	
Hosni:	I think it was about 1911.	
Andy:	Did he work as a writer?	
Hosni:	No. He worked for the Egyptian government.	
Andy:	What kind of literature does he write?	
Hosni:	Novels and short stories. He wrote three books called *The Cairo Trilogy*.	
Andy:	Where does he live?	
Hosni:	In Cairo.	
Presenter:	A 2 Listen and ask.	
	[REPEAT OF EXERCISE A1]	
Presenter:	A 3 Listen and answer.	
	[REPEAT OF EXERCISE A1]	

Exercise B

Refer students to Conversation 2. Point out that this conversation has the same basic pattern of question and answer.

1. Ask students to try to work out the questions and answers in each case. Monitor, but do not confirm or correct.
2. Play the conversation for students to check their ideas.
3. Play the conversation again. Pause after each question for students to answer as on the tape.
4. Play the conversation again. Pause after each answer for students to make the next question.

Put students in pairs to ask and answer about Selma Lagerlof. Monitor and assist as before.

Tapescript

Presenter: B 2 Listen and check.
Len: Who is your favourite writer?
Astrid: It's a woman called Selma Lagerlof.
Len: Who's she?
Astrid: She won the Nobel Prize for Literature in 1909.
Len: What kind of literature did she write?
Astrid: She wrote novels and short stories. She wrote a story called *The Wonderful Adventures of Nils*.
Len: What did she write about?
Astrid: She wrote about Varmland in the south of the country.
Len: Why did she write about Varmland?
Astrid: She loved the place. She was born there and she died there.

Presenter: B 3 Listen and answer.
[REPEAT OF EXERCISE B2]

Presenter: B 4 Listen and ask.
[REPEAT OF EXERCISE B2]

Exercise C

Set for pairwork. Refer students to the Skills Check to check their own work. Then feed back orally. Point out that there are two main kinds of verb here:
1. regular with final /t/, regular with final /d/ and regular with final /id/.
2. irregular.

Point out the contrast between the questions and answers about a living writer and a dead one, e.g.,

| What kind of literature | does he / did she | write? |

| He | writes | novels. |
| She | wrote | |

Drill the past tense forms, then prompt with the infinitive and get the past form.

Answers

Regular:

with final /t/	with final /d/	with final /id/
asked	answered	ended
looked	listened	tested
talked	lived	
worked	played	

Irregular:

be	was
win	won
write	wrote

Language and culture note

There is no rule of phonology that says an unvoiced consonant must follow an unvoiced consonant, or a voiced follow a voiced. Therefore, students need to be actually taught to say, e.g., *work* + /t/ and *live* + /d/. However, this regular past tense ending is often not discernible in the stream of speech because it is not exploded in front of another consonant, e.g., *I lived for five years in Germany. I worked down in the south.* Do not, therefore, spend too long on this, as it may encourage students to explode the consonant just to prove they know the rule, and thereby produce, e.g., *I live da for five years.*

Exercise D

Get a list of questions on the board as follows:
> *Who is your favourite writer?*
> *Is that a man or woman?*
> *How do you spell his / her name?*
> *Is he / she alive or dead?*
> *When was he / she born?*
> *When did he / she die?* (if dead)
> *What kind of literature did / does he / she write?*
> *What did / does he / she write about?*
> *Where did / does he / she live?*

Get students to interview you. Be prepared to answer the questions, ideally truthfully, with information about your favourite writer. Clearly, you may have to guess some of the information or say you don't know.

Set for pairwork. Monitor and assist. Get some of the best pairs to perform their conversations for the rest of the class.

Exercise E

Elicit a number of sentence patterns for the task as follows:
> *The most famous writer in my culture is …*
> *He / She was born in* (date) *in* (location).
> *He lives / lived in* (location).
> *He works / worked in* (location) */ as a writer …*
> *He / She writes / wrote* (kind of literature).
> *He writes / wrote about* (main topics).

Set the preparation for individual work, or put people into small groups from the same culture to choose a person. Monitor and assist.

Language and culture note

In English, you do not have to say whether a famous person is alive or dead. The form you choose for the main sentences, simple present or simple past, will tell the listeners this information.

Closure

Put students into groups – multicultural, if possible – to give their talk.

THEME 7 Sports and Leisure

General note
By the end of this theme, students should be able to hear and identify, in isolation and in context, the following words linked with sports and leisure. They should also be able to say them with reasonable pronunciation and use them in simple S V O sentences where V = present continuous, e.g., *She is reading a book.*

Sports	Leisure	Verbs
ball	beach	go
football	chess	listen to
stadium	cinema	play
surfing	film	read
swimming	mall	watch
tennis	music	
	radio	
	shopping	
	television	
	theatre	

Lesson 1: Listening

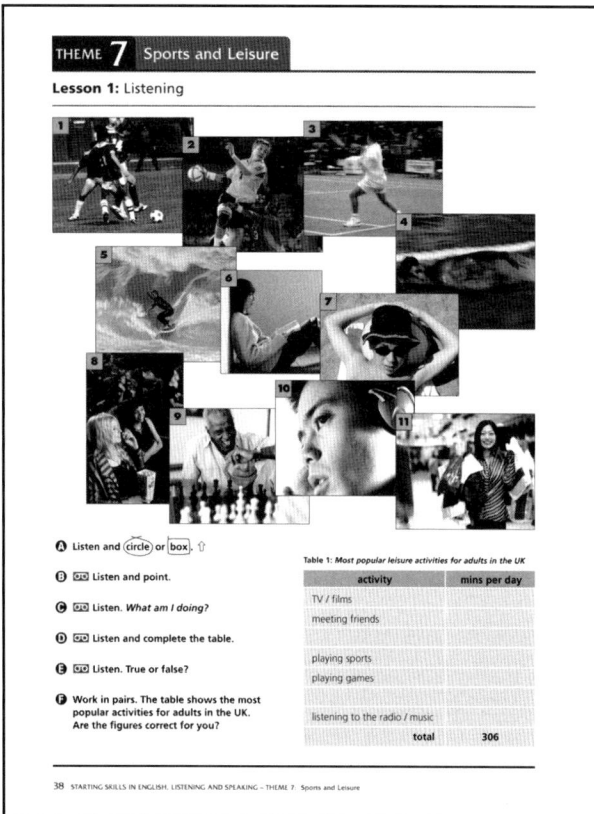

Introduction

Take in images / realia of the following:
  football
  tennis
  handball (if possible)
  swimming as a sport
  surfing
  a television
  a beach (Choose an acceptable image for your students.)

Also take in:
  a novel
  a Walkman, a radio
  a chessboard or chess piece (if possible)
  a music CD
  a video or DVD, ideally of a popular film

Say *We're going to talk about these things today*. Pin or stick the images on the board and arrange the other items on your desk. If students want to name the items, encourage this, but do not put students on the spot.

Point to all the items and say *Leisure. Not work. Leisure*.

Hold up each example of non-sport and ask *sport?* Elicit *No* in each case. Mix up the items and point at random to sports and non-sports. Each time say either *sport* or *leisure* with questioning intonation. Clearly, they should say *Yes* to *leisure* each time. After some time, add the word *activity* to *leisure*, i.e., start asking *leisure activity?*

Do not ask students to repeat the words, but allow them to do so if they wish.

Methodology note

These are useful hypernyms, as noted before. Saying something is *a sport* or *a leisure activity* narrows it down enough for people to be able to guess the actual item and help out the speaker.

Exercise A

Refer students to the pictures. Focus on items in the pictures from previous themes, including colours.

Say *Circle the sports*. Allow students time to circle the items.

Say *Box the leisure activities*. Allow time, as before.

Answers
Students can include all the sports items in one circle and all the leisure items in one box, or circle and box each item separately.

Exercise B

Hold up individual items from your realia, or point at them. Name them as follows:
> *going shopping*
> *going surfing*
> *going swimming*
> *going to the beach*
> *listening to music*
> *listening to the radio*
> *playing chess*
> *playing football*
> *playing handball*
> *playing tennis*
> *reading a novel*
> *watching a film*

As before, if students name the items correctly before you do, acknowledge that, but do not insist that students repeat each item.

Refer students to the pictures on the page. Say or play the tape with the words in isolation. Students point to the part of the picture.

Say or play the tape with the words in context. Students point to the correct picture.

Tapescript

Presenter:		Theme 7 Sports and Leisure
		Lesson 1
		B Listen and point.
Voices:		playing football
		going swimming
		playing handball
		reading a novel
		watching a film
		going surfing
		playing tennis
		going to the beach
		playing chess
		listening to music
		going shopping
Voices:		I love going swimming.
		He likes playing handball.
		Do you ever go surfing?
		I watched a fantastic film last night.
		Where can you play tennis in this town?
		I'm reading a good novel at the moment.
		Do you like going to the beach?
		I'm not good at playing chess.
		I always go shopping at the mall on Saturdays.
		I like playing football, but I'm not very good at it.
		My favourite leisure activity is listening to music.

Exercise C

Say *Look at the picture top left. What are they doing?* Elicit *playing football*. Repeat with at least three more of the pictures. Do not insist on full sentences or good pronunciation, just identification. Explain: *You are going to hear some sounds. What am I doing?* Play the first one as an example. Elicit *playing / watching football*. Point out that both answers are possible. Play the other sounds. Allow students to discuss answers before eliciting.

Answers

1. playing / watching football
2. surfing
3. watching a film
4. swimming
5. listening to music
6. playing tennis
7. shopping

Tapescript

Presenter: C Listen. What am I doing?
Sound effects:
1 extract from a football commentary
2 surf crashing on a beach
3 soundtrack of a film
4 sounds of a swimming pool
5 the noise of a Walkman as overheard
6 sounds of a tennis match
7 two people in a shop

Exercise D

Refer students to the table. Ask *What is the most popular leisure activity in the UK?* Elicit *watching TV / films*. Ask *What is in second / fourth / seventh place?*

Say the activity and ask for the position in the table.

Ask *What does 148 mean, for watching TV and films?* Elicit *That's the minutes per day.* Check how long that is in hours (about two and a half hours). Ask students if they watch TV films for two hours each day. Ask some more questions about the table.

Refer students to *playing games*. Ask *What does this mean?* Elicit *chess* or similar.

Ask students to suggest the missing leisure activities. Do not confirm or correct.

Answers

activity	mins per day
TV / films	148
meeting friends	85
reading	28
playing sports	14
walking, etc.	13
playing games	10
listening to the radio / music	8
total	306

Tapescript

Presenter: D Listen and complete the table.
Lecturer: What are the most popular leisure activities for adults in the UK? According to a recent survey, people over 16 in the UK spend most time watching TV or films. The average time is 148 minutes per day. That's almost two and a half hours each and every day. Meeting friends is in second place. Adults spend an average of 85 minutes on meeting friends, that's nearly an hour and a half. What's in third place? Playing football, perhaps, or listening to music? No, surprisingly, third place goes to reading. Yes, that's right, reading. People over 16 in the UK spend on average nearly half an hour reading each day – 28 minutes to be precise. That's all kinds of reading, novels, magazines and newspapers.
Playing sport of all kinds is in fourth place. Adults only spend about a quarter of an hour – actually 14 minutes – on playing sport. They spend nearly as long on playing board games like chess and draughts. Thirteen minutes, to be precise. In sixth place, we have walking. Adults spend 10 minutes walking each day.
Finally, in seventh place, we have listening to the radio or to music on a CD. On average, adults in the UK only spend 8 minutes listening to the radio or music.
These figures are for adults, for people over 16, in the UK. Do you think they are very different for adults in your country?

Exercise E

Put students into pairs. Make the following statement, then ask if it is *True* or *False*. Do not allow students to answer. Get them to tell their partner.

Watching TV or films is the most popular leisure activity for adults in the UK. (True)

Feed back. If necessary, explain. Get students to explain their answer. *It's in first place.*

Say or play the tape with the other questions, pausing after each one for students to discuss in pairs. Do not let students shout out the answer. Point out they must explain their answer as in the example.

Answers

Watching TV or films is the most popular leisure activity for adults in the UK.
True. It is in first place.

Walking is more popular than playing games.
True. It is in fifth place, playing games is in sixth place.

Meeting friends is in third place.
False. It is in second place.

Adults spend twice as long reading as playing sports.
True. 28 minutes to 14 minutes (You may have to explain *twice*.)

Adults spend over five hours on leisure activities.
True. 306 minutes

Adults spend over 50% of their leisure time watching TV.
False. It is just under 50% = 148 / 306.

Tapescript

Presenter: E Listen. True or false?
Voice: 1 Watching TV or films is the most popular leisure activity for adults in the UK.
2 Walking is more popular than playing games.
3 Meeting friends is in third place.
4 Adults spend twice as long reading as playing sports.
5 Adults spend over five hours on leisure activities.
6 Adults spend over 50% of their leisure time watching TV.

Exercise F

Set for pairwork. Monitor and assist. Feed back, getting people to give you ideas about themselves.

Closure

Ask students which leisure activity they like best. You can try asking them why, but it is unlikely that they have the language to explain. However, if you speak the students' language well, you can use a Community Language Learning approach, i.e., get them to tell you in their own language, then paraphrase it in simple English and teach them the way to express the idea.

Lesson 2: Listening

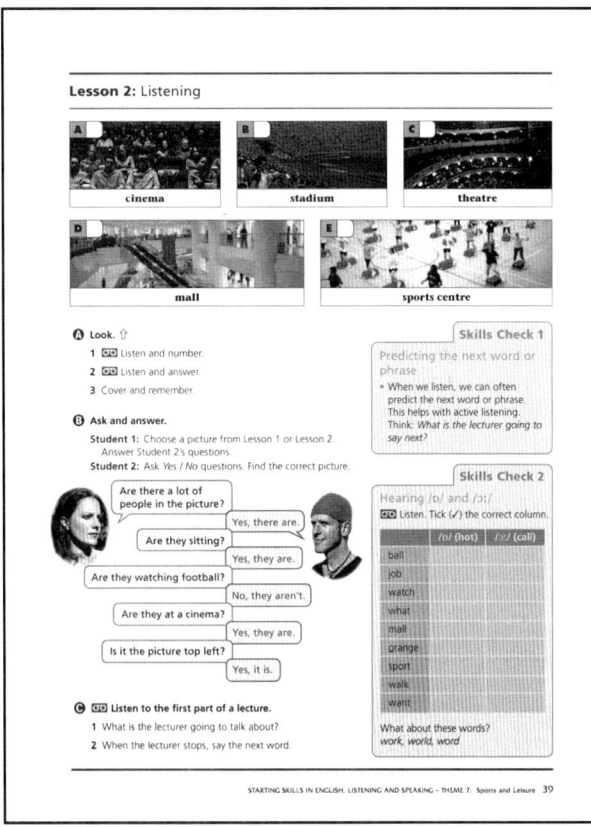

Introduction

Use the images and realia as before. On this occasion, say each word and get students to point or come up individually and touch or pick up the item.

Explain that students are now going to hear a short lecture. Remind them about preparing to listen – think: *What do I know? What will the lecturer say?*

Play the introduction. Ask students what they are going to hear about. Get them to identify the relevant pictures from Lesson 1. Ask them to think of possible words in pairs. Monitor and assist, modeling words that could be in the lecture.

Tell them to listen to the lecture and put them into two groups.

Set for individual work and pairwork checking. Play the rest of the lecture. Elicit the two groups and the answer to the lecturer's question at the end.

Answers

The two groups are *ball games* and *others*.
Students should have football, tennis and handball in Group 1.
They should have swimming and surfing in Group 2.

We say *play* with basketball because it is a ball game.
We say *go* with skiing because it doesn't need a ball and it ends in *-ing*.

Tapescript

Presenter: Lesson 2
Introduction
Part 1

Lecturer: There are many different kinds of leisure activities. One group of activities is sports. I'm not going to talk today about the other kinds of leisure activities, like reading and listening to music. I'm not even going to talk about watching sport on the television. I'm only going to talk about taking part in sports.

Presenter: Part 2

Lecturer: There are two main kinds of sport. Firstly, there are ball games. A ball game is simply a game played with a ball, for example, football, tennis or handball. In English, we use the verb *play* with these sports. So we say, for example, *I play football every Saturday* or *I can't play tennis* or *How do you play handball?*

The second kind of sport does not need a ball, for example, swimming or surfing. We do not use the word *play* with these sports. We say *go* instead. For example, we say *I go swimming on Sunday mornings* or *Where can you go surfing in this area?* Do you notice something about these sports? The words end in *-ing* – *swimming, surfing*.

So, how do you know which verb to use with a sport – *play* or *go*? Well, we use *play* with ball games, but we use *go* with sports which end in *-ing*. Which verb do we use with *basketball*? What about *skiing*?

Exercise A

1 Refer students to the five pictures. Set for individual work and pairwork checking. Play the tape. Students number the pictures. Feed back.
2 Play the first question as an example. Elicit an answer chorally. Continue with the other questions. Repeat, directing the question at individuals this time.
3 Ask students to cover their pictures and try to remember the location and details of each picture, especially the number of people and what they are doing.

Tapescript

Presenter: A 1 Listen and number.
Voice: 1 There are about ten people in this picture. They are walking. They are shopping at the mall.
2 There are thousands of people in this picture. They are sitting. They are in a very large stadium. They are watching a football match.
3 There are lots of people in this picture. They aren't standing. They are sitting. They are watching a film in a cinema.
4 There are a lot of people in this picture. They are doing step aerobics. They are at the local sports centre.
5 There are hundreds of people in this picture. They are watching a play in a theatre.

Presenter: A 2 Listen and answer.
Voice: 1 Is there a mall near here?
2 How often do you go to the theatre?
3 Does this place have a sports centre?
4 What is the name of the nearest football stadium?
5 What films are on at the cinema this week?

Exercise B

Refer students to the first picture in this lesson – the cinema. Ask the following *Yes / No* questions and get answers chorally.
Are there a lot of people in the picture?
Are they sitting?
Are they watching football?
Are they at a cinema?

Tell students you are thinking of a different picture from Lessons 1 or 2. Get them to ask you *Yes / No* questions about the picture to find out which one it is.

Set for pairwork. Monitor and assist. Feed back, getting some of the best pairs to perform their conversations in front of the class.

Remind students about the /ə/ sound at the end of, e.g., *picture*. Point out that we also use /ə/ with words ending in *-re*, e.g., *centre, theatre, metre*.

Exercise C

Remind students about listening to the introduction of a lecture and thinking: *What is the lecturer going to talk about?*

1. Play the first part of the lecture. Elicit ideas. Confirm and correct.
2. Refer students to Skills Check 1. Say you are going to test this idea with them. Play the first sentence as an example. Continue with the rest. Find out from students how they were able to predict correctly – basically it is the knowledge of the topic in general and the collocation of words in particular.

Tapescript

Presenter: C Listen to the first part of a lecture.
Part 1

Lecturer: There are two main kinds of leisure activities. The first kind is sports. I talked about sports last week. I'm not going to talk about sports activities today. I'm going to talk about the other kind of leisure activities.

Presenter: Part 2

Lecturer: We do some leisure activities with hundreds of other [PAUSE] people. For example, watching football in a [PAUSE] stadium, or watching a film in a [PAUSE] cinema, or watching a play in a [PAUSE] theatre. We do some leisure activities with one or two [PAUSE] friends. For example, watching television at [PAUSE] home or shopping at the [PAUSE] mall. We do some leisure activities alone, for example, reading a [PAUSE] book or listening to [PAUSE] music on a Walkman.

Closure

1. Refer students to Skills Check 2. Elicit and / or model the target sounds. Set for individual work and pairwork checking. Play the tape. Feed back, ticking the correct column, following the answers. Ask about the extra words.

Answers

	/ɒ/ hot	/ɔː/ call
ball		✓
job	✓	
watch	✓	
what	✓	
mall		✓
orange	✓	
sport		✓
walk		✓
want	✓	

Work, world and *word* all have the /ɜː/ sound despite the *or* letters in the middle.

Tapescript

Presenter: Skills Check 2
Listen. Tick the correct column.

Voice: ball
job
watch
what
mall
orange
sport
walk
want

2. Make the table of revision sounds and example words on the board. Check the pronunciation of the example words.
3. Elicit the words from the students and correct the pronunciation of the (underlined) vowel sound. Give students time to try to place the words in the correct column.

4   Say or play the target words from this theme which contain one of the sounds. Elicit the correct column to put it in.

Answers

six	three	eight	boat
/ɪ/	/iː/	/eɪ/	/əʊ/
film	beach	play	go
listen	read	radio	know
swim		stadium	

Tapescript

Presenter: Revision
Listen and put the words in the correct column.

Voice: beach
film
go
know
listen
play
radio
read
stadium
swim

5   Point out that the word play can be a noun (a perfomance at a theatre) and a verb (to do a sport).

Lesson 3: Speaking

Introduction

Use mimes to elicit the names of leisure activities. On this occasion, get students to say each word, chorally. Correct pronunciation as you go.

Ask students: *How do you spend your free time?* Elicit some ideas. Correct students so they are using the gerund form *-ing*, e.g., *shopping* or *going shopping*. When students have given you one or two activities, ask *Anything else?*

Ask a student who didn't mention any sports: *Do you like playing sports?* Elicit *Yes* and *No* answers.

Ask a student who said no: *What about watching sports?* Elicit answers.

Exercise A

Refer students to the pictures.

1 Elicit the sports. Get students to say the words individually. Correct pronunciation as you go. Check particularly the /ɒ/ and /ɔː/ sounds.
2 Elicit the non-sports. Repeat the procedure.
3 Elicit the places. Repeat the procedure.

Ask students: *How many people are there in the pictures?* Repeat for *men / women / children,* etc.

Answers
Possible answers – students can say just the sport / activity or the complete phrase at this stage.

1 playing football on a football field
2 surfing
3 playing chess
4 playing handball
5 reading a novel
6 listening to a Walkman
7 playing tennis
8 watching a play at a theatre
9 shopping at a mall
10 swimming
11 watching TV at home
12 watching a play at a theatre
13 watching football at a stadium

Exercise B

Refer students to the first picture (top left). Say *There are five children*. Repeat for the next picture. Elicit similar sentences about some of the other pictures. Refer students to the first picture again. Say *They are playing football*. Repeat for the next picture. Elicit similar sentences about some of the other pictures.

Refer students to the first picture again. Say *There are five children. They are playing football.* Indicate that there are two sentences here, one to your right, i.e., students' left, and one to your left. Bring your hands together and say *There are five children playing football*. Drill the joined sentences. Repeat for some of the other pictures.

Describe some of the pictures and get students to tell you which you are describing.

Put students into pairs for the activity. Monitor and assist. Feed back, getting a few students to give descriptions for the rest of the class to work out.

Exercise C

Ask students to look at the rebus conversation and try to work out what the people are saying. This should not be too difficult as you used the four questions in the introduction. Elicit ideas, but do not confirm or correct.

1 Play the conversation.
2 Play it again, pausing after each question for the students to answer, then play each reply for students to check.

Build up the questions and answers on the board. Show the use of the *-ing* form.

How do you spend your free time?		**Listening** to music.
Do you like	**playing** *sports?*	I **hate** playing sports.
What about	**watching** *sports?*	I **like** watching tennis and basketball.

Do not go into the reasons for the gerund use at this point. It will be dealt with in *Vocabulary and Grammar*. Drill the questions. Make sure students are using the falling intonation for the *How* questions and the fall rise for the *Yes / No* questions.

Get students to ask you the questions and give true answers. Get them to turn the information into an extended turn about you, i.e.,

He / She likes / loves … and …
He / She hates …

Tapescript

Presenter:	Lesson 3
	C 1 Listen.
Man:	How do you spend your free time?
Woman:	Listening to music.
Man:	Anything else?
Woman:	Watching television, reading.
Man:	Do you like playing sports?
Woman:	No, I don't. I hate playing sports.
Man:	What about watching?
Woman:	Well, I like watching tennis and basketball. What about you?

| Presenter: | C 2 Listen and answer. |
| | [REPEAT OF EXERCISE C1] |

Exercise D

1 Set for pairwork. Monitor and assist. Make sure students are using the correct intonation patterns.
2 Remind students about the mini-texts they made about you. Get students to construct mini-texts about their partner.

Closure

1 Elicit mini-texts from one of each pair.
2 Get students to do mimes of leisure activities for other students to guess.

Lesson 4: Speaking

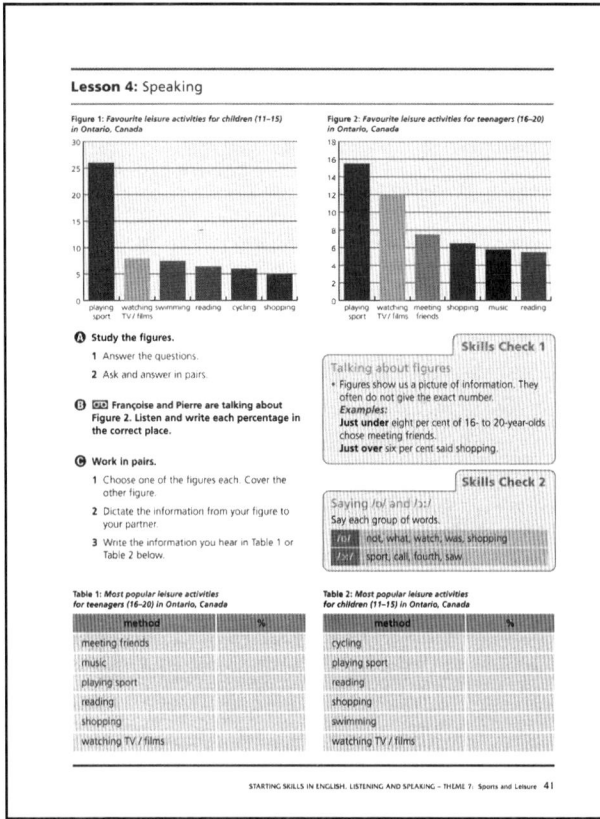

Introduction

Remind students of the mimes for different leisure activities. Do some yourself and get students to do some. Show a map of North America and point out where Ontario is in Canada.

Exercise A

Refer students to the two figures. Teach the phrase *bar chart*. Explain that a researcher in Ontario asked children:
  What is your favourite leisure activity?
Give an example result: *twenty-six per cent of 11- to 15-year-olds said 'playing sport'*.

1 Ask quick checking questions, e.g.,
    What do both figures show?
    Which figure is about teenagers aged 16 to 20?
    What is the other figure about?
    What is the favourite leisure activity for 11- to 15-year-olds?
    What about 16 to 20-year-olds?
    What percentage of 11- to 15-year-olds said 'shopping'?
    What about 16 to 20-year-olds?
    Which activities only appear in one of the figures?

2 Put students in pairs to ask and answer similar questions. Monitor and assist.

Ask students if they are surprised by any of the figures, or by any of the changes from 11- to 15-year-olds to 16- to 20-year-olds.

Exercise B

Set for individual work and pairwork checking. Play the tape. Give plenty of time for students to discuss. Feed back, ideally onto an OHT of Figure 2 for students. Write the percentages on. Get students to work out the other percentages and write them on.

Refer students to Skills Check 1 and work through the examples, drilling them.

Refer students to Skills Check 2. Drill the two sounds. Ask students for more words with the different sounds. From this course, the following are possible:
  /ɒ/: *hot, top, lot, got, bottom, job*
  /ɔː/: *sports, morning, north, taught, August*

Answers

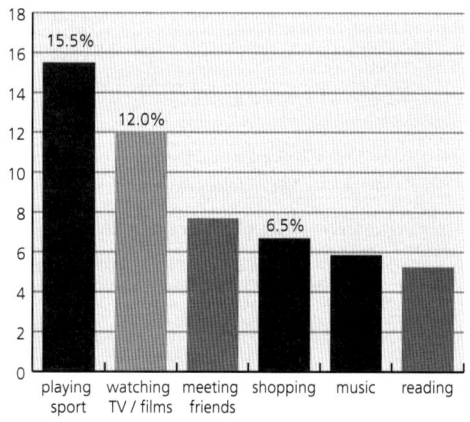

Tapescript

Presenter: Lesson 4
B Françoise and Pierre are talking about Figure 2. Listen and write each percentage in the correct place.
Françoise: What was in first place?
Pierre: Playing sport.
Françoise: What percentage of 16- to 20-year-olds chose that activity?
Pierre: Just under 16%. Say 15.5%.
Françoise: What was in second place?
Pierre: Watching films. Exactly 12%.
Françoise: What about shopping?
Pierre: Shopping was fourth at just over 6%. Say 6.5%.

Exercise C

Set for pairwork. Point out that the items in the tables are not in the correct order. Explain that they should number the items as they get the data and write in the percentages. Feed back, building up the tables on the board. Students may well have difficulties in working out the percentages because it is actually quite difficult. Point this out and allow discussion on the exact percentages.

Answers

Possible answers:

Table 1: *Favourite leisure activities for teenagers (16–20) in Ontario, Canada*

method	%
meeting friends	7.5
music	5.8
playing sport	15.5
reading	5.5
shopping	6.5
watching TV / films	12.0

Table 2: *Favourite leisure activities for children (11–15) in Ontario, Canada*

method	%
cycling	6.0
playing sport	26.0
reading	6.5
shopping	5.0
swimming	7.5
watching TV / films	8.0

Closure

Ask students to work in large groups and do a tally of the favourite leisure activities in the group. They should ask the question: *What is your favourite leisure activity?* and make a record of the answers. Then they should work out the percentage, quoting each point.

If you wish, you can take students right through to making and presenting the graph to the other group/s.

THEME 8 Nutrition and Health

General note
By the end of this theme, students should be able to hear and identify, in isolation and in context, the following words linked with nutrition and health. They should also be able to say them with reasonable pronunciation and use them in simple S V O sentences where O = countable or uncountable noun, e.g., *I like eggs / juice.*

Uncountable	Countable	Verbs
bread	drink (*n*)	drink
butter	eggs	eat
cheese	ice-cream	
chicken	potatoes	
coffee	sandwiches	
fish		
food		
fruit		
juice		
meat		
milk		
rice		
sugar		
tea		
water		

Lesson 1: Listening

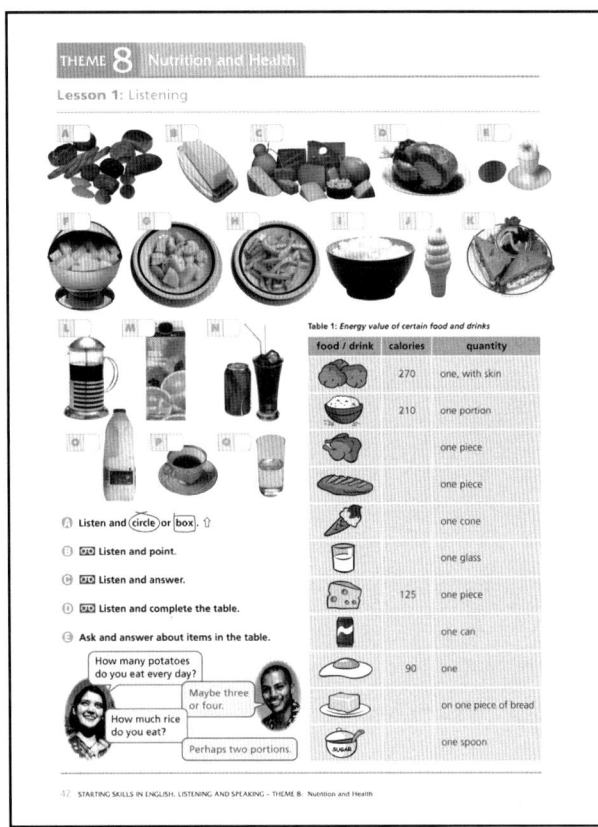

Introduction

Take in realia / packaging / pictures of as many of the following as possible:
   bread
   butter
   cheese
   chicken (as a food)
   coffee
   eggs
   ice-cream
   juice
   milk
   rice
   sandwiches
   sugar
   tea
   water

Pass them around and say the words as you do so.

Say *We're going to talk about these things today.* Arrange the items on your desk. If students want to name the items, encourage this but do not put students on the spot.

Pick up some items and say *food*. Pick up other items and say *drink*. Get someone to come up and try to arrange the items into food and drink. Pick up items at random and say *food* or *drink* and get students to say *yes* or *no*.

Say *You can eat bread ... and butter ... and eggs. You can drink coffee and tea and milk. Can you eat rice? Can you drink tea? Can you drink ice-cream?* Continue asking about other items at random.

Point out the usage of the nouns and the verbs again, highlighting the fact that *drink* can be a verb or a noun, i.e.,
   You can eat food.
   You can drink drinks.

Language and culture note

This activity may seem childishly simple, but in fact the way we divide comestibles into food and drink and the verb we use with each food (*eat / drink*) is language-specific. Even in English we have a few problems. Do we drink soup or eat it?

Methodology note

These are useful hypernyms as noted before. Saying something is a *kind of food* or a *kind of drink* narrows it down enough for people to be able to guess the actual item and help out the speaker.

Exercise A

Refer students to the pictures. Focus on items in the pictures from previous themes, including colours. Say *Circle the food*. Allow students time to circle the items. Say *Box the drinks*. Allow time as before.

Answers
They can include all the food items in one circle and all the drink items in one box, or circle and box each item separately.

Exercise B

Hold up individual items from your realia or point at them. Name them.

As before, if students name the items correctly before you do, acknowledge that, but do not insist that students repeat each item.

Refer students to the pictures on the page. Say or play the tape with the words in isolation. Students point to the correct picture.

Say or play the tape with the words in context. Students point to the correct picture.

Tapescript

Presenter: Theme 8 Nutrition and Health
Lesson 1
B Listen and point.

Voice:
1 cheese
2 butter
3 bread
4 chicken
5 coffee
6 eggs
7 ice-cream
8 milk
9 orange juice
10 potatoes
11 rice
12 cola
13 chips
14 sandwiches
15 sugar
16 tea
17 water

Voice 1: Would you like some coffee?
How about a cup of tea?
Do you take sugar?
Voice 2: I don't want milk, thank you.

Voice 1: Would you like some more potatoes or chips?

Voice 3: I had a cheese sandwich for lunch.
Voice 1: Did you? I had chicken and rice.

Voice 1: Could I have a glass of water, please?
Voice 2: Would you like a soft drink – cola?
Voice 3: Do you have any orange juice?

Voice 2: My favourite food is boiled eggs. I love them.

Voice 1: It's so hot. Do you fancy an ice-cream?

Voice 3: I'd like some bread and butter with my meal, please.

Exercise C

Explain that students are going to hear a number of questions. They must give true answers for them. Play the first question. Do not allow students to shout out an answer. Wait a few seconds then nominate a student. Continue with the rest of the questions. Elicit answers from several students in each case.

Tapescript

Presenter: C Listen and answer.
Voice: Do you like rice?
Do you have milk in tea or coffee?
Do you put butter on your bread?
Do you prefer tea or coffee?
Do you have eggs in the morning?
Do you want a cola?
What kind of potatoes do you like?
Do you like chips?
How many teas or coffees do you drink every day?
How much sugar do you have in your tea or coffee?
How much water do you drink every day?
What's your favourite ice-cream?

Methodology note

Students may struggle to answer some of the questions because they do not have the language. Allow other students to help them, but then make them give the answer themselves.

Exercise D

Refer students to the table. Explain that they are going to hear a short lecture about the information in the table. Ask students to discuss in pairs: *What is the lecturer going to say?* If students ask: *What does 'energy' mean?* etc., say *Do you think the lecturer will explain that?* The answer, of course, is yes!

Monitor and assist. Elicit some ideas, but do not confirm or correct. Students should be able to work out that the lecturer is going to talk about the foods and the calories in the food. Say *Listen to the introduction. Circle any words you hear.* Play Part 1 of the lecture.

Feed back, ideally onto an OHT of the table. Ask some questions about the meanings of the new words, i.e.,

Where do we get energy from? (Mime *energy*, if necessary.)
Why do we need energy?
How do we measure energy? (Mime the idea of measuring, if necessary.)
How much energy is there in a potato?
What about a portion of rice?

Refer students back to the table. Set for individual work and pairwork checking. Play Part 2 of the lecture. Feed back, building up the table on the board, or onto an OHT.

Methodology note

There are many words here that students will not be able to produce, or even understand fully, e.g., *measure*, *portion*, but they will get the general idea and learn an important lesson – that you never understand everything.

Answers

food / drink	calories	quantity
potatoes	270	one, with skin
rice	210	one portion
chicken	185	one piece
bread	160	one piece
ice-cream	150	one cone
milk	130	one glass
cheese	125	one piece
soft drinks	100	one can
eggs	90	one
butter	75	on one piece of bread
sugar	20	one spoon

Tapescript

Presenter: D Listen and complete the table. Part 1
Lecturer: Today I'm going to talk about food and drinks. Why do we eat food? Why do we drink drinks? Of

course, we eat because we like food, and we drink because we like drinks. But there is another reason for eating and drinking. We eat and drink to get energy. We need energy to do work. We need energy to do leisure activities. We get energy from food and drinks. Some food gives us a lot of energy. Some food only gives us a little energy. Today I'm going to tell you the energy value in certain foods and drinks. By the way, we measure energy value in calories. For example, one potato has about 270 calories. But one portion of rice has about 210 calories. So there is more energy in one potato than in one portion of rice.

Presenter: Part 2

Lecturer: Let's look at the energy value of some other foods. One piece of chicken has an energy value of 185 calories. But did you know that one piece of bread has almost as much energy? One hundred and sixty calories. And if you put butter on the bread, that's another 75 calories. Yes, that's right. One hundred and sixty for the bread plus 75 for the butter.

Do you like ice-cream? Well, one ice-cream has 150 calories. A glass of milk has slightly less at 140 calories. Sorry, I meant to say 130 calories. What about soft drinks, like cola or lemonade? Actually, they have fewer calories than a glass of milk. There are about 100 calories in a can.

There are no calories in tea or coffee. These drinks are mostly hot water. But one spoonful of sugar is 20 calories, so if you have two spoons and some milk, perhaps your cup of coffee has 60 or 70 calories.

Exercise E

Put students into pairs. Make the following statement, then ask if it is *True* or *False*. *One potato has more calories than one portion of rice.* (True)

Ask a few more questions of the same sort. Then ask the two questions in the speech bubbles. Elicit answers. Set for pairwork. Monitor and assist.

Methodology note

This is deep-end strategy in one sense, although it is unlikely that your students have never seen the countable / uncountable dichotomy in English. Point out the two questions – *much* and *many*, and the plural form in one case and the singular form in the other, but do not get bogged down in representing this at this stage. Just correct mistakes in the feedback without comment.

Closure

Ask students which food item on the page they like best. Ask if there is a favourite food or drink not on the page. Ask if they hate or can't eat / drink any item on the page.

Lesson 2: Listening

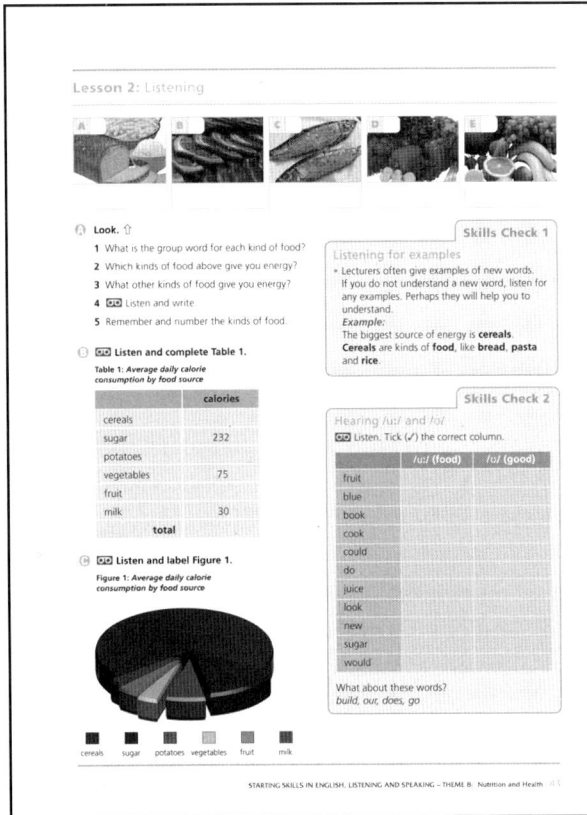

Introduction

Use the images and realia as before. On this occasion, say each word and get students to point or come up individually and touch or pick up the item. Refer students to the pictures. Ask them if they can name any of the items. Confirm any correct choices, but do not get other students to repeat.

Exercise A

1 Refer students to the five pictures again. Set for individual work and pairwork checking. Feed back, but do not confirm or correct.
2 Elicit ideas, but do not confirm or correct.
3 Repeat the procedure.
4 Point out the space for writing in under the pictures. Explain that they are going to hear part of a lecture and they should write the missing words in the correct place. Set for individual work and pairwork checking. Play the tape. If you think it is necessary, stop the tape after each section for students to think and, if appropriate, write. Do not feed back at this point as this may destroy the aural trace of the lecturer's words.

5 Ask students: *What is the main source of energy?* Elicit *cereals*. Point out that they should write *1* next to this source. Set for pairwork. Feed back. Point out that the lecturer mentions meat and fish – without spelling them, so check they have the correct spelling – but says they are not a major source of energy.

Work through Skills Check 1, highlighting places in the transcript where this happens.

Answers

 cereals

 meat

 fish

 vegetables

 fruit

Sources of energy should be numbered as follows:

1	cereals	5	fruit
2	sugar	6	milk
3	potatoes	7	meat
4	vegetables	8	fish

Tapescript

Presenter: Lesson 2
A 4 Listen and write.

Lecturer: In today's lecture, I'm going to look at the main sources of energy from food. As you know, we need energy to do work. But where do people around the world get the energy from? Rice? Potatoes? Chicken? Or something else?

Well, the biggest source of energy is cereals. Cereals are kinds of food, like bread, pasta and rice. We spell the word *cereals* C – yes, C not S – C-E-R-E-A-L-S. Cereals.

The second biggest source of energy is sugar. There is sugar in most food from the supermarket. We also put sugar in tea and coffee and in soft drinks, like cola.

The third biggest source of energy is potatoes. In many countries, people get most of their energy from this source.

In fourth place we have vegetables, like carrots and cabbage and tomatoes. People get energy from cooked vegetables. They also get energy from vegetable juice. By the way, there is an extra letter in the word *vegetables*. We say *vegetables* but we spell it V-E-G-E̱-T-A-B-L-E-S.

The fifth main source of energy is fruit – that's F-R-U-I-T. That's U I in the middle. Fruit is things like bananas, mangos, pineapples. People get energy from the fruit itself and from fruit juice like orange juice and apple juice.

Finally, in sixth place we have milk and milk products, like cheese and butter.

What about meat, like lamb and beef and chicken? There is some energy in this kind of food but meat is not a major source of energy in the world. The same is true for fish, like salmon and shark and cod. We eat a lot of fish in the world but we do not get a lot of energy from this source.

Exercise B

Refer students to Table 1. Ask them to guess the missing numbers. Get them to explain how they guess – the figure for each type of food is in order, so the first number must be the highest and the other number must be between the two on either side. Students should be able to explain this with their existing linguistic resources. Set for individual work and pairwork checking. Play the tape. Feed back, building up the table on the board.

Answers

	calories
cereals	1,189
sugar	232
potatoes	126
vegetables	75
fruit	65
milk	30
total	1,717

Tapescript

Presenter: B Listen and complete Table 1.

Lecturer: How many calories do people get every day from their food? The average daily amount is 1,717. People get most of this amount from cereals. The average daily amount is 1,189. One, one, eight, nine. As you know, sugar is in second place. The daily amount is 232 calories. Potatoes are third, at 126 calories. The calories from vegetables and fruit are very similar – 75 calories for vegetables and 65 for fruit. Finally, the average figure for milk is 30 calories.

Exercise C

Refer students to the pie chart. Point out that this is another way of showing the same data as in Table 1. It shows the breakdown in percentages. Ask students to guess what the percentages are from the size of the sections of the pie chart. Elicit ideas and help students if they are way off target, but do not confirm or correct. Set for individual work and pairwork checking. Play the tape.

Answers

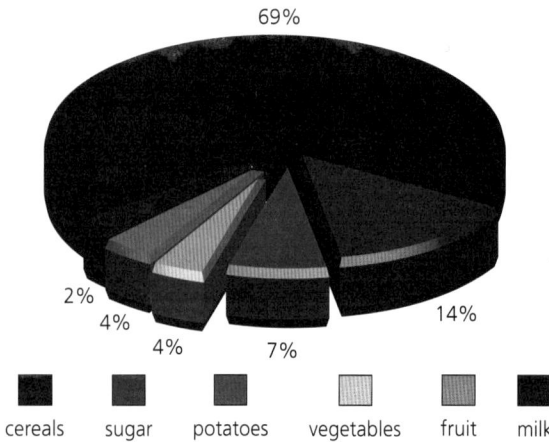

Tapescript

Presenter: C Listen and label Figure 1.

Lecturer: We can look at the information about daily calories in another way. On average, people get 69 per cent of their calories from cereals and 14 per cent from sugar – that's fourt<u>een</u>, not for<u>ty</u>. They get half that amount from potatoes – that's seven per cent, and four per cent each from vegetables and fruit. Milk provides only two per cent of the daily consumption.

Closure

Refer students to Skills Check 2. Elicit and / or model the target sounds. Set for individual work and pairwork checking. Play the tape. Point out the spelling patterns.

1. *oo* can be either sound.
2. *ui* is usually /uː/, but it is /ɪ/ in *build* and its derivatives.
3. *ou* can be /ʊ/, but has other sounds in, e.g., *our* and *house*.

Point out also that *do* has an /uː/, but in the third person it is /dʌz/.

Answers

	/uː/ food	/ʊ/ good
fruit	✓	
blue	✓	
book		✓
cook		✓
could		✓
do	✓	
juice	✓	
look		✓
new	✓	
sugar		✓
would		✓

Tapescript

Presenter: Skills Check 2
Listen. Tick the correct column.
Voice: fruit
blue
book
cook
could
do
juice
look
new
sugar
would

Lesson 3: Speaking

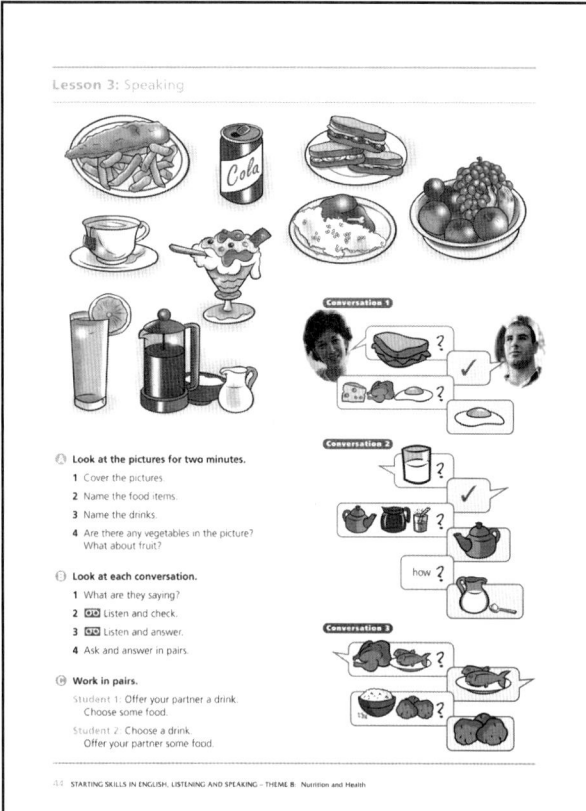

Introduction

Use mimes to elicit the names of food and drinks, e.g.:
- cutting bread
- putting butter on bread
- putting something inside to make a sandwich
- making a cup of tea with a tea bag and adding milk and sugar
- making a pot of coffee – in the traditional way for your students, if you know it
- pouring out a glass of water from a tap
- squeezing juice
- pouring milk from a bottle
- opening a can and pouring cola
- catching a fish
- killing a chicken (if you can bear to do it!)
- putting an ice-cream in a cone
- eating an apple
- eating a carrot – perhaps like a rabbit
- eating a boiled egg

Put students in pairs to play the same game.

Exercise A

Follow the instructions as written. Feed back, checking that as many students as possible prove they know the names of the food items.

Exercise B

1 Set for pairwork.
2 Play Conversation 1.
3 Play Conversation 1 again, pausing for students to answer.
4 Set for pairwork.

Repeat the procedure for Conversation 2 and 3.

Tapescript

Presenter: Lesson 3
B 2 Listen and check.
Conversation 1
Voice 1: Would you like a sandwich?
Voice 2: Oh, yes, please.
Voice 1: What kind would you like?
Voice 2: Egg, please.

Presenter: Conversation 2
Voice 1: Would you like something to drink?
Voice 2: Yes, please.
Voice 1: Coffee, tea or a cold drink?
Voice 2: Tea, please.
Voice 1: How do you like it?
Voice 2: Milk and one sugar, please.

Presenter: Conversation 3
Voice 1: Would you like chicken or fish?
Voice 2: Could I have the fish, please?
Voice 1: Certainly. Would you like rice or potatoes with that?
Voice 2: Potatoes, please.

Presenter: B 3 Listen and answer.
[REPEAT OF EXERCISE B2]

Exercise C

Drill the main questions from the three conversations as follows:
> *Would you like a sandwich?*
> *Would you like chicken or fish?*
> *Would you like something to drink?*
> *How do you like your tea?*
> *Would you like rice or potatoes with your fish?*
> *Could I have the fish, please?*

Drill the main answers as follows:
> *I'd like some tea, please.*
> *Milk and one sugar, please.*

Set the activity for pairwork. Monitor and assist.

Closure

1. Elicit mini-texts from one of each pair.
2. Get students to do mimes of food and drink for other students to guess.

Lesson 4: Speaking

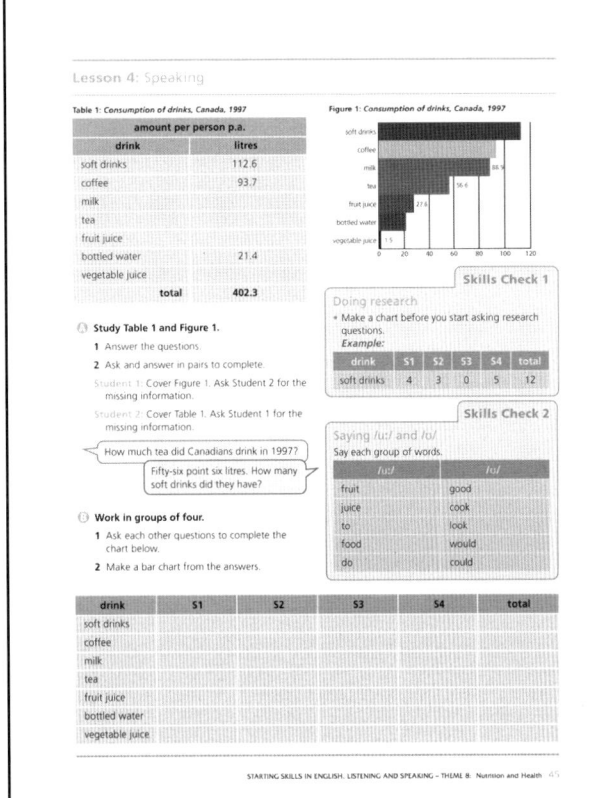

Introduction

Remind students of the mimes for different foods and drink. Do some yourself and get students to do some. Remind students where Canada is.

Exercise A

Refer students to Table 1 and Figure 1. Teach the word *consumption* – drinking or eating; in this case, drinking. Teach the expression *per annum* and the abbreviation *p.a.* Teach the word *bottled*, if necessary.

Explain that researchers in Canada found out the total amount of each kind of drink in 1997 and divided it by the population – average consumption per person per annum.

Explain that there are just over 30 million people in Canada, so they drank just over 3,360 million litres of soft drinks in 1997 (3,360 million / 30 million = 112 litres per person). So the average person drank 112.6 litres of soft drinks in 1997. That is about a third of a litre, or one can, every day (112.6 / 365). Ask students if they drink that much every day.

Repeat the process with the information about coffee = 30 million x nearly 100 litres = 3,000 million litres of coffee.

Explain that there are about 250 millilitres in a cup – 1/4 of a litre. So, the average Canadian drank nearly 100 litres = about 400 cups, or just over one a day. Ask students if they drink that much every day.

Teach *more / less*.

1   Ask quick checking questions about the information in the table and the figure. Point out that the answer may be in either the table or the figure, e.g.,
    How much coffee did the average Canadian drink in 1997? (93.7)
    What is 21.4? (The amount of bottled water that the average Canadian drank in 1997.) Do not worry if they can't say this very well!
    Which was more popular – bottled water or fruit juice? (Fruit juice)
    How do you know? (It is above bottled water, and the drinks are in order of popularity.)
    How much milk did Canadians drink in 1997? (88.9 litres)

2   Work through the questions in the speech bubbles. Point out that all the words need *How much?* Drill, including the intonation pattern. Put students in pairs to ask and answer questions. Monitor and assist.

Ask students if they think the figures are the same for their country / countries.

Methodology notes

1 The word *consumption* would normally be above the level of false-beginner students, but its surrender value is much higher in academic English than it would be in general English.
2 Averages are a basic component of academic research. Students must be competent and confident about calculating averages.
3 This is further deep-end strategy on the countable / uncountable issue.

Exercise B

Refer students to Skills Check 2. Drill the two sounds. Ask students for more words with the different sounds. From this course, the following are possible:
/uː/ *flew, true, blue, clue, drew, student*
/u/ *took, book, woman*

Work through Skills Check 2. Point out the importance of organising information as you collect it. Drill the two questions in the speech bubbles. Point out that we need to say *cups* and *glasses*, etc., with *How many?* Elicit *cans* for soft drinks and *bottles* for water.

1 Refer students to the table at the bottom of the page. Set for group work. Give plenty of time for students to ask each other questions. Monitor and assist.
2 Make sure students understand how to make the bar chart. If you wish, hand out graph paper for ease of construction. Monitor and assist.

Closure

Feed back, displaying the best bar charts.

Word Lists: Thematic

STARTER	THEME 1 Work and Business	THEME 2 Science and Nature	THEME 3 The Physical World
afternoon (n)	accountant (n)	black (adj)	bottom (n)
answer (n and v)	bank (n)	blue (adj)	centre (n)
ask (v)	computer (n)	brown (adj)	coast (n)
begin (v)	court (n)	cloud (n)	country (n)
day (n)	doctor (n)	cold (adj)	east (n)
end (v)	engineer (v)	colour (n and v)	island (n)
evening (n)	factory (v)	grass (n)	lake (n)
first (adj)	hospital (n)	green (adj)	left (adj)
hour (n)	hotel (n)	grey (adj)	map (n)
last (adj)	job (n)	hot (adj)	mountain (n)
listen (v)	lawyer (n)	orange (adj)	north (n)
month (n)	office (n)	red (adj)	river (n)
morning (n)	receptionist (n)	sky (n)	south (n)
night (n)	secretary (n)	snow (n)	top (n)
now (adv)	shop (n)	sun (n)	town (n)
question (n)	start (v)	tree (n)	village (n)
read (v)	typist (n)	white (adj)	west (n)
right (adj)	want (v)	yellow (adj)	
student (n)	work (n and v)		
test (n and v)			
time (n)			
today (n)			
week (n)			
write (v)			
wrong (adj)			
year (n)			

THEME 4
Culture and Civilization

adult (n)

baby (n)

boy (n)

child (n)

female (adj)

friend (n)

girl (n)

male (adj)

man (n)

old (adj)

people (n)

person (n)

teenager (n)

woman (n)

young (adj)

THEME 5
They Made Our World

bicycle (n)

boat (n)

bus (n)

car (n)

come (v)

drive (v)

fly (v)

go (v)

motorbike (n)

plane (n)

road (n)

sail (v)

ship (n)

taxi (n)

train (n)

walk (v)

THEME 6
Art and Literature

architect (n)

architecture (n)

art (n)

biographer (n)

biography (n)

get (v)

give (v)

literature (n)

meet (v)

move (v)

novelist (n)

paint (v)

painter (n)

painting (n)

play (n and v)

playwright (n)

poem (n)

poet (n)

sculptor (n)

sculpture (n)

see (v)

send (v)

stop (v)

take (v)

teach (v)

write (v)

THEME 7
Sports and Leisure

ball (n)

beach (n)

cinema (n)

film (n)

football (n)

leisure (n)

mall (n)

music (n)

play (v)

radio (n)

shopping (n)

sport (n)

stadium (n)

surfing (n)

swimming (n)

television (n)

tennis (n)

theatre (n)

watch (v)

Word Lists: Alphabetical

THEME 8
Nutrition and Health

bread (n)
butter (n)
cheese (n)
chicken (n)
coffee (n)
drink (n and v)
eat (v)
egg (n)
fish (n)
food (n)
fruit (n)
ice-cream (n)
juice (n)
meat (n)
milk (n)
potato (n)
rice (n)
salad (n)
sandwich (n)
sugar (n)
tea (n)
vegetable (n)
water (n)

accountant (n)
adult (n)
afternoon (n)
answer (n and v)
architect (n)
architecture (n)
art (n)
ask (v)
baby (n)
ball (n)
bank (n)
beach (n)
begin (v)
bicycle (n)
biographer (n)
biography (n)
black (adj)
blue (adj)
boat (n)
bottom (n)
boy (n)
bread (n)
brown (adj)
bus (n)
butter (n)
car (n)
centre (n)

cheese (n)
chicken (n)
child (n)
cinema (n)
cloud (n)
coast (n)
coffee (n)
cold (adj)
colour (n and v)
come (v)
computer (n)
country (n)
court (n)
day (n)
doctor (n)
drink (n and v)
drive (v)
east (n)
eat (v)
egg (n)
end (v)
engineer (v)
evening (n)
factory (v)
female (adj)
film (n)
first (adj)

fish (n)
fly (v)
food (n)
football (n)
friend (n)
fruit (n)
get (v)
girl (n)
give (v)
go (v)
grass (n)
green (adj)
grey (adj)
hospital (n)
hot (adj)
hotel (n)
hour (n)
ice-cream (n)
island (n)
job (n)
juice (n)
lake (n)
last (adj)
lawyer (n)
left (adj)
leisure (n)
listen (v)

literature (n)
male (adj)
mall (n)
man (n)
map (n)
meat (n)
meet (v)
milk (n)
month (n)
morning (n)
motorbike (n)
mountain (n)
move (v)
music (n)
night (n)
north (n)
novelist (n)
now (adv)
office (n)
old (adj)
orange (adj)
paint (v)
painter (n)
painting (n)
people (n)
person (n)
plane (n)

play (n and v)
playwright (n)
poem (n)
poet (n)
potato (n)
question (n)
radio (n)
read (v)
receptionist (n)
red (adj)
rice (n)
right (adj)
river (n)
road (n)
sail (v)
salad (n)
sandwich (n)
sculptor (n)
sculpture (n)
secretary (n)
see (v)
send (v)
ship (n)
shop (n)
shopping (n)
sky (n)
snow (n)

south (n)
sport (n)
stadium (n)
start (v)
stop (v)
student (n)
sugar (n)
sun (n)
surfing (n)
swimming (n)
take (v)
taxi (n)
tea (n)
teach (v)
teenager (n)
television (n)
tennis (n)
test (n and v)
theatre (n)
time (n)
today (n)
top (n)
town (n)
train (n)
tree (n)
typist (n)
vegetable (n)

village (n)
walk (v)
want (v)
watch (v)
water (n)
week (n)
west (n)
white (adj)
woman (n)
work (n and v)
write (v)
wrong (adj)
year (n)
yellow (adj)
young (adj)

Lesson 2: Listening

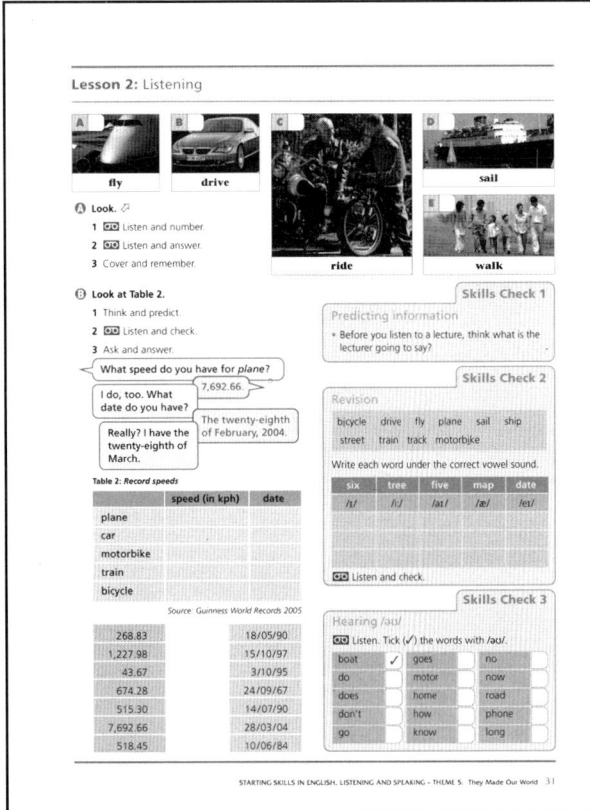

Introduction

Quickly revise the key words from the unit, in isolation and in context. Get students to point at the correct place on the page. Use a variety of sentence patterns, e.g.,

There is / are …
I can see …
The cars are on the road.
The people are walking.

Ask *Where can you see planes / boats / cars?* etc. Elicit *In the sky / On a lake / On a road.* Avoid *train / track.*

Do not worry if students give you other answers, e.g., *At an airport / In a port / In a car park.* Accept correct answers, but do not teach these points to others unless they specifically ask.

Teach the difference between *road* (between villages, towns and cities) and *street* (inside villages, towns and cities). Draw a sketch map to reinforce the point.

Exercise A

1 Refer students to the five pictures. Set for individual work and pairwork checking. Play the tape. Students number the pictures. Feed back.
2 Play the first question as an example. Elicit an answer chorally. Continue with the other questions. Repeat, directing the question at individuals each time.
3 Ask students to cover their pictures and try to remember the location and details of each picture. Teach them *far* to go with *left* and *right*, e.g., *on the far left*. They can test each other in pairs.

Answers

1 A 5
   B 1
   C 2
   D 4
   E 3

Tapescript

Presenter: Lesson 2
          A 1 Listen and number.
Voice: 1 drive
      2 ride
      3 walk
      4 sail
      5 fly

Presenter: A 2 Listen and answer.
Voice: Do you drive to college?
      Do you have a bicycle?
      Do you walk a lot?
      Can you fly a plane?
      Where can you sail in your country?